IDEAPRESS
PUBLISHING

Proudly printed in the United States by Ideapress Publishing.

Ideapress Publishing | www.ideapresspublishing.com

All trademarks are the property of their respective companies.

Cover Design by Faceout Studios

First Printing: January, 2019

Cataloging-in-Publication Data is on file with the Library of Congress.

ISBN: 978-1-940858-76-0

Special Sales

Ideapress Books are available at a special discount for bulk purchases for sales promotions and premiums, educational institutions or for use in corporate training programs. Special editions, including personalized covers, custom forewords and bonus content are also available. For more information, email info@ideapresspublishing.com

Limitless

How to Ignore Everybody, Carve Your
Own Path, and Live Your Best Life

Laura Gassner Otting

Contents

For Arnie Miller, who taught me to bring all of myself to everything I do.

Introduction

If you're anything like me, you've spent most of your professional life working your ass off, positioning yourself *just so*, reaching for that résumé-building assignment that would put you in line for that next big promotion and that next big job.

If you're anything like me, you've followed everybody's advice about what success should look like, and about the fastest path you can take to fill all the right checkboxes along the way.

And if you're anything like me, once you've filled all those checkboxes along someone else's path to someone else's success, you've turned around and wondered why, when everything was so "full," it still felt so empty.

Well, you're not alone. Nearly two decades ago, I felt the same way. I was firing on all cylinders, but I was bored, unsatisfied, empty. On paper, my career was a bright shining light. And yet I was miserable. I felt like a fraud. I was encircled, bounded, contained by the limits of expectations, by what I was supposed to do and how I was supposed to feel.

I lacked consonance.

But a janitor at NASA, back in 1962, didn't.

Perhaps you've heard about him. The (possibly apocryphal) story goes like this: The Space Race was rocketing into full swing when President John F. Kennedy visited Cape Canaveral for the first time.

While viewing the base, he noticed a janitor cleaning a mop and he interrupted the tour to introduce himself.

"Hello, I'm Jack Kennedy," said the president (or so the story goes). "What kind of work are you doing here?"

The janitor replied, "I am helping put a man on the moon."

That janitor wasn't constrained by other people's definitions of success. He was doing work that mattered to him in pursuit of goals that mattered to him. *What* he did matched *who* he was. And that made him limitless.

I, on the other hand, was not.

Why was my story so different from the janitor's? What did he know that I did not? I had done everything right, so why did it still feel like I got it all wrong?

The Trouble with Leaning In

My problem back then wasn't my pursuit of success. Like you, I was hardwired to follow whatever path was necessary to accomplish my goals. No, my problem was my perspective. I was focusing on the wrong problem, so my solution wasn't working.

I thought I was solving for the problem of finding the fastest, most expedient path to the idea of success handed to me by parents and teachers and mentors and friends. But I was mistaken. Rather than trying to achieve this external, widely accepted version of success, I should have been looking for success that actually worked for *me*—specifically, uniquely, quirkily me.

I soon learned that this was not just my problem, but a problem that many of us share. The problem isn't how we *achieve* success, but how we *define* success.

We are told early and often how to be successful. Books like *Lean In*, which took the professional world by storm in 2013, encourage us to follow one particular path: claw our way to the spotlight, wrangle the fast track, demand the big shot. This advice champions the path of assertiveness, of boldness, of driving to the top of the organizational chart with as much speed and determination as we can muster. It encourages us to put ourselves smack-dab in the center of the deal flow.

Well, "leaning in" may be a good path for many, but it isn't the right path for all. As it turns out, even Sheryl Sandberg's own research shows that despite all this leaning in, not that much has changed in terms of equalizing pay or even securing offices for women in the C-suite. In fact, as the research points out, "Progress continues to be too slow—and may even be stalling."[1]

And it's not just women who are limited by this myopic, unflinching definition of success. We are all limited, women and men both, to measuring our progress by how fast and how high we climb. We are limited by the imaginations and burdens of others. We are limited by their opinions about who we are and where we belong. We are so limited by checking off the boxes of other people's versions of success that we forget to determine our own. And in these limits, we lose ourselves.

I bought into it at first. Leaning in and other such approaches to this all-encompassing, Machiavellian pursuit of professional success worked for me—until they didn't. I began to bristle at the narrowness of this one-size-fits-all route to success. I'd had that type of success, and now I wanted something else entirely. I required purpose. I demanded meaning. I needed to live a life of consequence.

And I didn't need that life to be consequential with a capital C. I had no plans to win a Nobel Peace Prize or discover the cure for cancer. I didn't need the world to mourn my death with a full-page obituary in the *New York Times*. But I needed my life to feel consequential to *me*, to inspire the people I love, and to reflect the causes I hold dear.

I needed my work to matter.

---

1 McKinsey & Company and LeanIn.Org, "Women in the Workplace 2017," https://womenintheworkplace.com.

I've come to learn that in order for your working life to feel right for you, it has to actually *be* right for you. I would like you to stop being held back by others. I need you to determine what is right for you, first and foremost, and to set new goals that reflect your one-of-a-kind path. I want you to become limitless.

And in order to do that, you will have to align your work and your personal self. In order to become limitless, you must achieve consonance.

Becoming Limitless

Simply defined, *consonance* is when *what* you do matches *who* you are (or want to be). You achieve consonance when your work has purpose and meaning for *you*. This meaning might be professional, societal, or personal. It might be actual (some concrete, immediate change in your life) or aspirational (a subtle shift in your intentions).

Consonance is easy to recognize, but it takes intention to achieve. Realizing it is missing is often easier than figuring out how to get it.

Over the course of interviewing hundreds of leaders from the corporate, nonprofit, and public sectors, I saw over and over again the damage caused by a lack of consonance, by the disconnect between purpose, action, and that external view of success. And I saw that true success comes from a combination of four particular elements that allow individuals to carve their own path, do their best work, and live their best lives. Exploring these four foundational elements of *calling*, *connection*, *contribution*, and *control*—introduced in detail in chapter 1 of this book—will help you break through your external and internal limits. Understanding how these elements align for you, personally and professionally, will allow you to become limitless.

This book begins with the premise that the only definition of success that counts is yours and yours alone—and that the only way to be truly limitless is to journey along your very own life's path. I encourage you to stop giving votes to the people in your life who shouldn't even have a voice. Only you get to decide. And only you can then determine how much of each of those four elements *you* need in order to be in consonance and lean in to what matters to *you*.

My approach is based on a twenty-year career of studying, recruiting, and stewarding leaders through major career changes. It is based on my own path throughout my career, in my workplace, and for myself—and on the stories of many others who are discovering their own path, in their own individual way. We will explore some of those stories here.

We will also examine what being limitless can look like, why you may be struggling to achieve it, and how you can identify and prioritize—with confidence—the various drivers for your own life. We will explore actionable steps that can help you decide whether your unique path to consonance will require changing your career, changing your workplace, or changing yourself. And if you feel like you don't have the privilege to make a change right now, this book will give you some tactics to employ in the meantime so that you can be best positioned when the time is right.

That janitor at NASA back in 1962 had a calling. He wasn't an engineer, a math savant, or an astrophysicist, but he recognized that he played a crucial role in maintaining the environment necessary for his NASA colleagues to achieve their goals. He saw a clear connection between his daily tasks and goals and his organization's critical mission. The values and achievements of his organization inspired him and contributed to his sense of pride. He had control over how much he was able to connect his everyday work to his calling and the contribution that it made to his life. He wasn't limited by someone else's definition of success. He knew that everyone plays a role that matters, regardless of whether you hold a broom or a calculator. In short, he was limitless—because he had discovered his consonance.

Now, let's go find yours.

PART ONE
THE CONSONANCE CRISIS

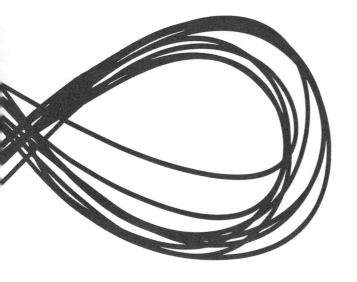

Chapter 1

Why We're Stuck

Army Captain Joshua Mantz knew exactly what was happening as the bullet struck on that hot, dusty day in Baghdad in April 2007. He knew exactly what was happening as the blood rushed into his stomach and his chest cavity, the way it does when the body is making a last-ditch effort to protect its vital organs. And he knew exactly what was happening as he thought about his family, took his last breath, and died.

For a full fifteen minutes after being shot by an enemy sniper, Josh Mantz flatlined. All the while, the medics continued to administer CPR, do-or-die drugs, and a rapid succession of jolts from a defibrillator. Then, miraculously, Josh's pulse returned, faintly at first but gradually growing stronger. He came back from beyond the brink of death—and with his brain capacity fully intact. From that point on, he was faced with figuring out why.

It might be considered trite—this idea that once you've stared death in the face, the next step is to figure out what it all means. (Hey, don't blame me; you're the one who just picked up a book about living your best life.) But in hours of conversations with Josh I've learned one thing. And no, it's not whether he saw a bright light at the end of a tunnel. (He didn't. I asked.) What I learned is this: the void is often clearer than the solution. We know when things aren't right; we just don't always quite know what's wrong.

When you're confused or unsatisfied in your work or your life, the void is all too obvious. Solving for the void is where things become difficult.

Lucky Is a State of Mind

When Josh returned to military service after an arduous physical recovery, he attacked his work with such fury that he was awarded the best assignments, earned an early promotion to major, and threw himself into a Crohn's disease flare-up so brutal that it nearly killed him again. He had to slow down before he shut down. He had to step back a bit and gain some clarity. But as Josh will tell you, he isn't so good at doing things halfway.

Josh knew that if he was to step back from his meteoric, high-paced military career, the only career he'd ever sought or known, he would have to step back all the way. So he did just that. He left the military entirely and joined—what else?—the fastest-growing private-sector company in the world: Tesla. (I told you he wasn't good at halfway.)

The pace felt like combat, the mission was world domination, and the founder's focus was singular and unwavering. Tesla was a comfortable and familiar environment, to say the least, and one that would nurture Josh's full-press pursuit of success.

But Josh kept getting requests to speak in public about his experience in Iraq and the months and years that followed his death. People wanted him to talk about recovery, to talk about trauma. He would work sixteen-hour days at Tesla building leadership development and companywide employee engagement programs and then race to the airport to catch a flight and give a speech—before racing back for work the next day. It was, as he calls it, an "allurement"—an unavoidable passion, something he couldn't not do. But this lifestyle was untenable. He was living two lives, each foot in a different speedboat, both going in opposite directions. He lacked consonance.

Everything Josh was doing mattered. It was important work. Helping those with trauma was undeniably life-saving and obviously close to his heart. And it was thrilling work. Tesla was growing at a rate that was garnering front-page stories around the world, and his work was teaching him heady, valuable lessons. Each day people told him how amazing he was, how amazing his career was, how amazing his life was. But he didn't feel so amazing.

While Josh had plenty of allurement in his life, he didn't have alignment. Rather than clarity, there was confusion. Rather than consonance, there was dissonance. He was bombarded with conflict: doubts about who he was, what he cared about, how he spent his time, and the vision of the world he wanted to create. He was stressed-out and empty—all while being told, again and again, that he was the luckiest guy on earth.

If the "luckiest guy on earth" feels as though his purpose is in doubt and he's spinning out of orbit, then surely the rest of us have absolutely no chance, right? Well, actually, no. If who you are doesn't match what you do, regardless of how this manifests, it's time to figure out why.

Josh needed to dedicate serious thought and effort to his direction in life. He felt pulled to pursue his true calling of revealing the truth behind trauma and what really happens when soldiers come back from war. So he left Tesla to try his hand in the healthcare arena, thinking that a management position at Acadia Healthcare—one of the largest health providers in the United States—would help him achieve his calling to help those who had suffered from sexual abuse, opioid addiction, school shootings, and an endless list of other trauma-related challenges. But he was still confronted by working within a traditional—and, from his perspective, broken—treatment model.

Josh dove into the depths of his soul and scraped the bottom of his bank account as he figured out how to move forward in a way that would work for those he wanted to heal, as well as for himself. He needed to be in a place professionally where he could see the connection between the work he was doing and the solution he sought. And he needed, for his own health, to do it in a way where he could control and scale the pace of how he worked and whom he treated.

Josh spent a year and a half—the hardest months of his life, he says, including those when he had to learn to walk again—writing his highly acclaimed autobiography, *The Beauty of a Darker Soul*, in which he describes his death, his journey back through life, and his efforts to create a leadership training and consulting company , Asymmetric Minds. Asymmetric Minds focuses on how leaders can integrate psychologically adverse experiences to drive optimal performance at the individual and organizational levels. In short, he's helping people and companies understand how to turn traumatic experiences into strengths, not just scars.

Josh's search for personal consonance produced a win–win scenario: He has discovered greater fulfillment in his working life, and countless people can now benefit from his breakthrough approach to leadership. His path to becoming limitless came snatched from the jaws of death. The good news is that yours won't be nearly as harrowing.

So let's get started.

What Is Consonance?

Consonance is the sense of frictionless belonging, of momentous stride, of core relevance. It is a guiding force that reveals how your work (whatever that may be) contributes to your overall life's plan. It connects your daily activities to the success of those around you, and gives you clarity about why you—*specifically you*, in that seat, in that office, in that box on the organizational chart—matter. Consonance is not just purpose writ large (and lofty). It's *your* purpose, freely and clearly defined by you, and put into action through awareness of and alignment with your life's plan.

Consonance looks different for everyone. And it's ever-changing, evolving as we age and pass through life's various stages and adjust our priorities. Yours will be unique to you. The four elements that make up your consonance, however, are fixed.

The Four Elements of Consonance

The elements of consonance are *calling, connection, contribution*, and *control*, and you will need to have at least some of each of the four.

Wait, what? You need to have *all four* elements to have consonance? Yep, you do. Without all four elements, it is impossible to go from confusion to clarity and to feel confident and limitless in your choices.

So, what exactly do each of the four elements of consonance entail?

Calling is a gravitational pull towards a goal larger than yourself—a business you want to build, a leader who inspires you, a societal ill you wish to remedy, a cause you wish to serve.

Connection gives you sightlines into how your everyday work serves that calling by solving the problem at hand, growing the company's bottom line, or reaching that goal.

Contribution means that you understand how this job, this brand, this paycheck contributes to the community to which you want to belong, the person you want to be, or the lifestyle you'd like to live.

Control reflects how you are able to influence your connection to that calling in order to have some say in the assignment of projects, deadlines, colleagues, and clients; offer input into shared goals; and do work that contributes to your career trajectory and earnings.

You can think of it in this way: Until we are able to *control* how our *connection* and our *contribution* influence and are influenced by our *calling*, we will continue to be limited in the confidence we have and the choices we make.

Rohit Bhargava was an author, speaker, and college professor who recognized a problem that needed solving: He didn't like the way traditional publishers treated and compensated authors. As an author, he felt out of control and at the mercy of the publishing industry. This was hampering his ability to do his best work. Rohit wanted to do what he loved—publish books so that great ideas could take flight.

Seeing an opportunity to build a successful business around a fairer model, Rohit launched his own imprint, IdeaPress. He now offers innovative thinkers and experts (like Yours Truly) an alternative to the less favorable contracts offered by bigger publishers. Building his own business has allowed Rohit to better align his work with his overall purpose (his *calling*), to *contribute* to the life he wants to live, and to have complete *control* over his destiny.

Renee Koczkodan is a hairdresser who worked for eighteen years in other people's salons, where she felt stuck under the thumb of one owner after the next—tolerating leaky business models, supporting bad management practices, and handing over way too much of her earnings. Then one day Renee heard about an opportunity to rent a chair in a start-up salon where she could have more control over her own profit margin. She figured out what she needed to earn, and then spent the rest of her time training to become a yoga instructor and a health coach. The changes she made gave her *control* over her working life and allowed her to follow her *calling*: to build a holistic portfolio of enabling beauty, inside and out.

Like Josh, Rohit and Renee are both examples of how someone can achieve consonance in his or her life. Yet each took a different approach to becoming limitless; there is no single formula that allows everyone to find consonance.

If you're going to clear the way to becoming limitless in your personal and professional life, you'll need to ignore everybody and carve your own path. Combining and balancing the four elements to suit *your particular version* of consonance will give you the confidence to do it.

Many Versions of Consonance

Each of us values *calling, connection, contribution,* and *control* differently, and your assessment will change as your career evolves. Some of us want and benefit from a little of each element, a relatively even balance. Others front-load one or two, sacrificing a bit of the elements that matter to them less in order to increase those that matter more. You can achieve your specific individual version of consonance—alignment between your daily work and your energy, passions, and skills in pursuit of larger goals—by being conscious of and building up at least some of each element.

The weight you assign each element will vary at different stages of your career, and these weights will define the direction that your career takes. But be forewarned: your path to becoming limitless is a work in progress. Having all of some elements and none of the others is often necessary for short-term gain at different career stages. Paying your dues in the early years, for example, comes with precious little *connection* (unless you count gophering coffee, filing papers, and other such glamorous tasks), but loads of *contribution* (in the form of networking and acquisition of skills, though not usually income). Later on, *control* (the flexibility to set your own hours or influence your income stream) might matter more to you than *calling* (whether or not you love the company deep down in your bones).

Josh recognized in himself the importance of that first element of consonance, *calling*—an overarching motivation, a goal to reach, a problem to solve, an issue to overcome, a bottom line to meet, a brand or leader to love. His calling is broadening leadership capacity through a better understanding of trauma. But what allows him to be limitless, what gives his calling shape and trajectory, is the second element: the *connection* he feels about how his daily tasks have an impact on the achievement of his overall mission. Feeling connected to something bigger—whatever your motivation, whether for community, company, or country—can be deeply fulfilling.

Throughout his career, Josh placed all the weight on calling and connection. What allowed him to become limitless was finally rounding out the third and fourth elements of consonance: *contribution* and *control*. Josh learned that he needed to have an awareness of the contribution that his efforts were making—how redefining trauma, providing mental and emotional healing, and developing leadership qualities in others could be what he did in his nine-to-five, not just his five-to-nine. Doing work that provides the lifestyle you require (both monetarily and healthwise) allows you to let your work be part of your fuller self.

Becoming limitless also required Josh to be certain that he had some level of control over which practitioners worked alongside him and which leaders he trained in this new paradigm. Having control over your working environment—the work you do, the people with whom you collaborate, the career path you forge, your earning potential—satisfies a basic human need to have agency in one's personal world.

Josh stepped *way* outside of expectations and the norm, shirked the customary definitions of success that were all around him, and carved his own path. In doing so, he aligned his energy, his mission, and his talents. He became limitless.

The Wrong Path

Being limited sucks. We recognize limits when we are constrained by them, and we know how good being limitless can feel. We often yearn to be limitless, but, like Josh, we often get it wrong before we finally get it right. Why is this? What gets in our way and stops us from living our best lives?

It comes down to four insidious, unreachable ideals—impossible goals set against the background of sunset-gazing, flower-crowned young women with perfectly beach-waved hair, lounging in a viral social media meme: *passion, purpose, happiness,* and *balance*.

Follow Your Passion: The World's Worst Advice

You are probably surprised to discover that part of the reason we get things wrong so often is simply that we have been given bad advice since the dawn of time: *Follow your passion!* That advice—the spoken-word illegitimate sister of the *Live! Love! Laugh!* tattoo—sounds all well and good, and maybe it even looks pretty in a scrolly font. It tantalizes with fleeting euphoria … before it packs a wailing uppercut of disappointment.

As anyone who has ever followed their passion will tell you, your passion will rough you up. It will disappoint you. It will play hard to get. It will gut you—and maybe your bank account, too. Doing something about which you are passionate is the holy grail, and by all means, let's get there. But the promise of bliss, however Instagrammable, is ephemeral and insufficient. While following your passion might get you on the road, it doesn't provide a road map.

Rather than following your passion, you need to invest in your passion—by devoting your time, treasure, and talent to leaning into the goals that you set for your particular life plan. Gary Hirshberg, founder of Stonyfield Farms—a leading organic yogurt company that gets all its milk from local dairy cooperatives—didn't limit his passion to running a single farm. Instead, he leaped into the business sector and started a purpose-driven campaign, building his ideals into a company that advocates not just for healthy, locally-sourced yogurt but for environmental justice.[2]

Investing in your passion requires an understanding of what gives you consonance. Before you can invest in your passion, you must discover your own mix of calling, connection, contribution, and control—and learn how each of these elements matters to you

---

2 Stonyfield sells 13.3 percent of the yogurt in North America and gives 10 percent of its profits to environmental causes. See Jim Cornall, "Lactalis Buying Stonyfield from Danone for $875M," *Dairy Reporter*, July 2, 2017, https://tinyurl.com/ybq4dkmr, and "Stonyfield Farm," Big Purpose Big Impact, accessed October 3, 2018, https://tinyurl.com/y6u8osut.

individually. We will address these elements one by one, and consider how to achieve your best mix, in later chapters.

The Purpose Fallacy

Even if you manage to escape the passion trap, you will probably spend some time mucking about with another long-held trope that is the darling of college career centers: the one that conflates purpose with *calling*, not taking into account the other three elements—*connection*, *contribution*, and *control*—that are necessary to make you limitless.

How many times have you been admonished to seek out a higher calling, to perform some service for others, to prioritize the greater good over your own needs or desires? *Do your job, make your money, and volunteer on the side*, they advised. *Get your purpose outside of work*, they counseled. So you learned to accept a misguided model, where purpose can only mean service to others and your day job should be primarily for income generation.

The pursuit of cause and cause alone is no guaranteed panacea. Nonprofit and volunteer work is not the only way to have a calling and to feel purpose. Sure, working towards an important and meaningful goal—like Josh, who wants to help people understand and become empowered by trauma—can be part of your purpose. But Josh also made sure to take into account how building a business could help him pursue his own personal, career, and financial goals. Knowing your purpose without taking into account all four elements of consonance doesn't make you limitless. In fact, it does the opposite.

Sure, it can feel good to endeavor to save the whales, or cure cancer, or stem childhood hunger. But those who satisfy their pursuit of purpose only with such worthy causes often find themselves suffering the same frustrations—especially when the whales are still dying, cancer still kills, and children still go to bed with empty bellies. They have the same feeling that something is missing, and now they probably have smaller paychecks to boot. They have purpose, but they still feel empty.

That doesn't mean you need to abandon purpose entirely. In fact, I would argue quite the opposite: that you should integrate purpose and calling into your life plan *now*.

You see, we've also been programmed to think purpose has to wait. In 2017, I was sitting backstage at a US military base in Japan, waiting to give a talk about how people transitioning out of the armed services can find meaningful work. I heard myself introduced as the "expert on nonprofits" who would come onstage and talk about non-profit work as "the thing people do after they've made their money, and a nice thing to keep back-burnered for when the time comes." As you can imagine, I lost my mind and came out heartstrings a-blazin'! I wasn't about to tell a room full of people in the military—people who had self-selected as service-minded—to wait years before pursuing their next career of purpose, to delay that mission of service until they did some other, less meaningful job. That idea needed to be corrected ASAP, PDQ, and on the double.

Retired Lieutenant Colonel Amy McGrath was the first female Marine Corps fighter pilot. She flew eighty-nine combat missions in the Middle East and returned home to teach government to young cadets at the US Military Academy. Compelled by what she saw after the 2016 elections as a lack of leadership in our current political structure, she didn't wait for her teaching career to be over to pursue more purpose. Instead she left her position at West Point to run for US Congress.

Military or not, waiting is bananas. The time to insert purpose into your work is not when you are done working, but as soon as you figure out what you want that purpose to be.

What's the worst thing about the purpose fallacy? It has created a false flag, signaling that service can be real only if it comes with a heaping helping of martyrdom. This traditional thinking sends people to the nonprofit sector to don the white hat and save the world. Purpose, after all, should serve something bigger than just us, right? So the sector demands that those seeking a life of service take a haircut on our salaries, our benefits, our perks. It persuades us to prostrate ourselves to the Gods of Poverty in order to feel like any of it matters.

Sure, meaningful work can—and often does—involve service beyond self. But I know plenty of people working in corporate jobs who feel fully inspired by their work. I know just as many working on behalf of nonprofits who feel as though they are spinning their wheels and lacking connection to how their daily tasks have an impact on a higher calling. Imagining self-sacrifice in pursuit of service to others as the only purpose that could possibly have meaning is what got us into this mess.

There's nothing wrong with nonprofit work if that is truly what is right for you. After all, I spent the majority of my career in service to that sector, and I discuss these options throughout this book. But the deeper we dig ourselves into the hole of that sort of binary thinking—*service is good, self-interest is bad*—the more we find ourselves equating purpose with self-sacrifice.

I'm here to tell you that's a load of bunk. We can feel purpose in our lives *and* make a sustainable income. We can do well *and* do good. These concepts need not be at war with one another.

Happiness as a Stand-In

As if the demands for passion and purpose weren't muddying things enough, we've also confused happiness at work with fulfillment. It's supposed to be work, not fun, right? So, if we are happy, doesn't that mean we've gotten away with something—we've found a loophole?

We feel happy at work if we are given great benefits, like free lunch and foosball in the breakroom; if we have an easy commute; or if our best friend is in the cubicle next door. These things are good for morale, so human resources managers are constantly looking for the newest, fanciest perk to trot out as part of the employment proposition.

Here's the problem with that: Any company can hire a clever HR manager who can find the next big thing, whether it's free dry cleaning, dog-friendly offices, or Workout Wednesdays. These things build community, they are good for recruiting, and they look compelling as notices on the back of the door in the bathroom stall. But simple pleasures never last; soon enough, you'll be looking for the next bright, shiny retention object. And nothing is better for retention than feeling like the work you do really matters.

We've thrown our expectations about happiness at home into this confusion as well. We presume that work should be hard and home should be easy. But what if that formula is reversed? What if home is where the heartache is? Well, it's easier to change jobs than relationships, so we nitpick around the edges of life, poking holes in our work instead. We decide that the problem is the job, when often what is needed is a change at home.

A limitless life path requires congruence between the two—your work world and your home world—such that the values you live in each world bolster each other. Happiness can be a byproduct of being limitless, but being limitless is not a byproduct of happiness.

The Ephemerality of Work–Life Balance

Lastly, we heave upon ourselves the lofty and unattainable burden that, in the perfect state of nirvana, we should always be able to balance our professional and personal lives. In fact, I would argue, the very fact that we define ourselves differently at home and at work and then try to balance the two means we aren't balancing anything at all. Rather, we are pitting one side of ourselves against the other and thus limiting our ability to achieve balance in either.

Being limitless doesn't come from balance—which is lucky, given that the achievement of balance is only ever fleeting at best. Instead, it comes from alignment of the energies used both at work and in life towards the same overarching goals.

Feeling out of kilter doesn't come from doing too much; it comes from the in-betweens of the "too much," from the mental energy it takes to switch from one mindset to another in the space of time it takes you to commute from home to work or vice versa, or from an external-facing client meeting to the internal work of creating invoices and back again. Don't believe me? Just consider the rapid-fire costume changes your mind and heart experience in order to ricochet from the person you are at work to the person you are at home.

Rather than looking for balance between two opposites, strive to become limitless by aligning yourself along one set of standards which you can use in both settings. You might even find that the more aligned your energy and your values are with your daily work, the more your daily work spills across into other parts of your life. When what you do in the office resembles how you live outside of the office—and when you don't have to shed your true, comfortable skin and put on a brave face whenever the clock strikes nine a.m. or five p.m.—you are beginning to see consonance in your life. Friends and colleagues merge into "frolleagues." And none of it feels like work, because it's all about a magnetic pull that comes from deep inside of you: the expression of who you are through what you do.

*　*　*　*　*

Now that you understand what being limitless is—and what it isn't—here are my questions for you: What would being limitless feel like for you? What do you need to change in order to get there? And what will be the cost if you don't?

If you don't know, you're about to find out.

Chapter 2

The Value of
Questioning Limits

Purpose. Engagement. Consonance. These are all lofty words that—for far too long, and by far too many sources—have been assigned only platitudes and unrealistic goals. It can feel like these ideals are for other people, at other times, in other work. But times are changing, and demographic shifts are heralding a new dawn in the expectations around how work should fit into our lives.

For this, we can thank the millennial generation.

Now, I know everyday news stories seem to blame millennials—those born in the 1980s and 1990s—for pretty much everything that goes wrong in the workplace. But millennials are forcing a conversation about work that has never been had before. As they flood the workforce,[3] employee attitudes are shifting. Society as a whole is rethinking what a job should and shouldn't be.

---

3 By 2025, millennials will make up 75 percent of US workers. Debra Donston-Miller, "Workforce 2020: What You Need To Know Now," *Forbes*, May 5, 2016, https://www.forbes.com/sites/workday/2016/05/05/workforce-2020-what-you-need-to-know-now/.

Technological advances that herald transparency, speed, and limitless possibility have emboldened millennials to expect more from their work sooner and to demand a seat at the table so that they can contribute in bigger ways. No longer satisfied with holding jobs that are separate from the rest of their lives, avid hikers want to work for companies with sound environmental policies; young feminists look for companies that intentionally promote professional development for women; and weekend warrior athletes seek out offices where the shared snacks are healthy and the company hosts outdoorsy outings. These millennials have redefined workplace norms. Together, they are forcing corporations to develop more appealing employment propositions.

But it's not just millennials pushing for more. As more and more baby boomers—the children of JFK, RFK, and MLK—near retirement,[4] they are going back to their roots in 1960s social justice and searching for encores that matter. And Gen Xers are not to be left out. Finding themselves caught between raising children and nursing aging parents, Gen Xers are looking for work that contributes to managing these demands rather than working against them.

Everywhere, at every age, people are waking up and asking, "Is this all there is?"

A Multigenerational Push: Why Now?

Viewers of the 2018 Super Bowl were treated to something even more surprising than the underdog Philadelphia Eagles beating the powerhouse New England Patriots: The television advertisements were different than in previous years. Normally funny, sometimes even with raunchy bits designed to promote products like beer and

---

4 Starting in 2011, a staggering ten thousand baby boomers turned sixty-five every single day; this will continue until the very youngest ones blow out their birthday candles in 2029. Russell Heimlich, "Baby Boomers Retire," Pew Research, December 29, 2010, https://tinyurl.com/y9sjys2s.

cars, the ads that year featured a significant shift to storytelling arcs about the ethos of the companies making those products. Organizations across the globe were vying to be regarded as the most values-driven, banking on the recent trend of Americans looking to feel better about where they spend their consumer dollars. Gone was the scantily clad Paris Hilton eating a sloppy burger on the hood of a convertible; board members had realized that the best way to increase shareholder value was to demonstrate concern about the environment, inequality, educational access, women's rights, families, and LGBTQ issues.

Why did this happen? And why now?

In 2016, the United States elected a president whose demeanor, discourse, and policies have propelled the country into a crisis of values. Yet we also live in the age of global leaders like Justin Trudeau of Canada and Emmanuel Macron of France (to name just two), who form a growing wave of younger, anti-establishment politicians eager to put the ways of the past behind us. When asked why he chose a cabinet that was 50 percent made up of women, Trudeau stated, "Because it's 2015."[5] In June 2018, incoming Spanish prime minister Pedro Sánchez upped the ante by filling two-thirds of his cabinet with women.[6] This stark contrast between competing leadership styles and values has forced a conversation—about what we stand for as a society, and about what we want from the eighty thousand hours spent at work over the course of a typical life.

Our need for our work to matter is being front-burnered, succumbing to increased pressure from the youngest workers and the oldest. Becoming limitless means defining *calling, connection, contribution,* and *control* in your life according to their relevance for

---

5 Frederic Bisson, "Justin Trudeau: Because it's 2015!" YouTube video, November 4, 2015, https://www.youtube.com/watch?v=LLk2aSBrR6U.

6 Raphael Minder, "Spain's New Leader Forms Government with Almost Two-Thirds Women," *New York Times*, June 6, 2018, https://tinyurl.com/ybv6v92p.

you at each age and at every life stage. And this is manifesting in the workplace in different ways for different types of workers. Here are some examples.

Taking Pride in One's Work

Millennials want to work for companies that they believe in, that make them proud. In fact, an overwhelming majority of millennials identify purposeful work as a key factor in choosing among multiple employment options. Companies that focus on bringing significance into the workplace benefit from more engagement among workers, and engaged workers are far more productive for the companies and causes they serve.[7]

Pride of purpose enables leaders to motivate employees, companies to connect with customers, and workers to understand their role in and contribution to the larger system.

Transitioning for Greater Connection

More and more, midcareer professionals looking to gain new skills are transitioning to the nonprofit sector. Because nonprofits simply do not have the luxury of hiring as many specialists as companies in the corporate sector, "generalist professionals" wear many hats, and each staffer handles more responsibilities. Corporate professionals who once were pigeonholed as financial services employees, for example, can take on roles in the nonprofit sector that include finance, operations, and administration.

Therefore, by transitioning to a different industry or sector, midcareer professionals are often able to connect directly, through a broader portfolio of work, to the causes they want to serve.

---

7   According to a 2013 Gallup study of 1.4 million employees, engaged workers are 22 percent more productive for those companies. Susan Sorenson, "How Employee Engagement Drives Growth," *Workplace* (blog), Gallup.com, June 20, 2013, https://www.gallup.com/workplace/236927/employee-engagement-drives-growth.aspx.

Experimenting with Entrepreneurism

Experienced executives are proving to be the best entrepreneurs in today's economy. The average entrepreneur isn't actually a college student creating the next Facebook in an Ivy League dorm room, but a thirty-nine-year-old with plenty of work experience.[8] Further, experienced workers-turned-entrepreneurs are five times more likely to be successful than their younger counterparts,[9] partly because they can self-finance, but also because they have had the time to experiment with different professional paths, roles, and responsibilities.

Older entrepreneurs know better what kind of work brings out their best talents and can therefore be less limited in how they leverage their talents to achieve success.

Seeking Alignment

Professionals of all ages are looking for more alignment between who they are and what they do. Purpose-driven corporate cultures tend to have a different perspective on the metrics that really matter, because they allow employees to bring their whole self to work, and not just be the drone trained to address the task at hand. A culture that values purpose doesn't award martyrdom badges for all-nighters or champion face time with the boss, but rather focuses on what should actually count: real progress toward the shared goal of the cause, the community, or the company.

With this communal respect for the important goals comes an understanding that taking time away from the office doesn't

---

8   According to a recent study by the Ewing Marion Kauffman Foundation. Carmine Gallo, "New Studies Reveal the Ideal Age to Start a Business, and It's Not in Your 20s," Inc.com (February 14, 2018), https://www.inc.com/carmine-gallo/new-studies-reveal-ideal-age-to-start-a-business-its-not-in-your-twenties.html.

9   Ibid.

necessarily take away from the ability to achieve in the office. In fact, environments that encourage the alignment of work and life—where there is fluidity between the friend/family member/community member who exists outside of work and the employee who enters the office each day—find that their workers tend to bring more of themselves to the task at hand.

Employees who pursue personally significant endeavors can uncover ideas that are complementary to the mission of the organization and which improve their company's bottom line. A great idea generated because a staff member saw it put into action during a PTA event is still a great idea, yet it would have been missed if the employee had felt inhibited about discussing the very PTA meeting that made him or her late for work last Friday.

Whole selves beat half selves every day of the week.

Making "Retirement" Meaningful

Millennials aren't the only ones searching for meaningful work that instills a sense of pride. Baby boomers, in particular, want to explore a purpose outside of themselves and find meaning in the final professional chapter of their lives.[10] Baby boomers, not ready to put their hard-earned toolboxes on the shelf to gather dust, are seasoned and wise; they know that their formidable skills can be game-changing. When faced with more free time and longer lifespans than ever, this generation is looking for ways to create a second career—paid or unpaid—that focuses on giving back.

*   *   *   *   *

---

10 In a recent study by Stanford University and Encore.org, one-third of Americans over the age of fifty—nearly 34 million people—stated that they were seeking to fill their time with some purpose beyond just the self. A. Colby and J. Emerman, "Kick Back or Live With Purpose? Why Choose?" Encore.org, May 22, 2018, https://tinyurl.com/y93enymj.

At the heart of these conversations is a need for our career to fit into our larger life plan. The outraged, the unfulfilled, and the disappointed—of all ages—simply want more these days: more justice, more fulfillment, more satisfaction. We are living in a time of upheaval and uncertainty. We are witnessing and participating in unprecedented political and social change, experiencing the growing pains that come with revolutionary technological advances, and facing the challenges that come with increased interconnectivity at home and around the globe. Every day, millions of people wake up feeling—with unprecedented acuteness—as though the work we do needs to matter.

We're all seeking consonance in our lives, even if we don't know it yet.

Believe me, I see it again and again. And I don't just talk about rejecting limits and finding consonance from the standpoint of the thousands of nonprofit, corporate, and government leaders I've studied, recruited, and stewarded though massive transformations in their careers. When it comes to these lessons, I've carved that very same path myself.

My Own Path to Becoming Limitless

I found myself at my first career crossroads at age twenty-five. I had been working as a presidential appointee in the White House, and had just helped design and launch the volunteer national service program AmeriCorps, delivering on President Bill Clinton's signature campaign promise to give young people a way to exchange community service for college tuition. Soaked to the bone with hope and optimism, I decided that the best use of my embarrassment of connections—and my utter dearth of actual job skills—was to go into nonprofit executive search, connecting powerful and accomplished mission-driven people with careers that I felt were vital to creating a better world.

So I did what any self-respecting, mildly arrogant idealist would do: I went to the best in the business. And when they hired me, I was delighted.

I began learning from the brightest minds how to perform a somewhat artful task: applying science to gut reaction. I learned how to use well-tested methods to gather data that proved (or disproved) our instincts about candidates' strengths and weaknesses. I learned how to hold my own and provide invaluable advice to professionals who were usually much older and much more established and successful than me. I learned how to make assessments and draw conclusions based on a couple of hours in interviews, and to test those conclusions through twenty or more hours of additional interviews, performance assessments, and reference checks.

My colleagues were at the top of their game. They were at the vanguard of cause-driven executive search, defining how it should be done, with an enviable client roster of the most well-respected brands from the nonprofit, foundation, and education sectors. We were working to make the world a better place.

But it wasn't working for me. Something was missing.

The Missing Link(s)

As discussed in chapter 1, the first step is to determine what value you place on each of the four elements of *calling, connection, contribution,* and *control*. For each of us, the weights assigned will vary, leaving us with a particular balance usually defined (to some degree) by age and life stage.

At that point in my young career, I definitely had *calling*: I was serving this higher purpose to which I'd assigned paramount value. I was making the world a better place.

And I had *contribution*—living my values through my work, learning at race pace from the best and the brightest, expanding my knowledge as fast as my network, and even making decent money (at long last).

But I was not in consonance.

I was still quite young, and I was assigned to a box on the organizational chart that did not earn me access to senior staff strategy meetings. To be clear, I was the lowest of the low: senior vice president of smiling and dialing. My job entailed picking up the phone and calling some well-known boldface name—usually a high-flying, radically intimidating person. I would try to get that person to spill open his or her Rolodex and nominate rock-star friends and colleagues for the searches we were undertaking on behalf of our clients. But make no mistake: a hyper-idealistic cubicle drone is still a cubicle drone.

While I was eager for exposure and hungry for new challenges, choosing me to travel for client meetings didn't benefit the company's bottom line, so I was rarely able to see my behind-the-scenes work put into action. After all, with my limited experience, I wasn't able to provide great insight to the client, and at my tender age, I didn't lend an impression of gravitas or brilliance to the traveling team. For the most part, I was still wearing my mother's hand-me-down office clothes from the 1980s; my shoulder pads, while enormous, didn't shout, "MVP!"

So I had no *connection*.

Furthermore, I had no say in what projects landed—or didn't land—in my lap. My role was to take on whatever tasks the management team deemed the best use of my time, regardless of how inspired I was about a particular client or how much fresh energy, networking, or knowledge I could bring to the project. I was unable to advocate for myself, to get placed on the assignments that would get me noticed when it came time to reward associates with promotions. Sometimes I was the right person for the job, but mostly I was just the most proximate warm body with space in my portfolio for a new assignment.

So I had no *control*.

Even though I understood that profits and losses dictated these decisions, I began to feel that my position was hindering me from contributing my best work and reaching my full potential. I began to develop a nagging feeling that the work could be done better and faster—with more authenticity, more integrity, more flexibility, and more transparency—not just for me, but for our clients, too.

My misgivings about the executive search process grew stronger, but I was working with "the best in the business," so I chalked it up to just needing to pay my dues. *You're just young,* I thought. *It will feel better once you move up the corporate ladder.* As time went by and I rose through the ranks, however, I couldn't shake the feeling that this environment was not going to allow me to do the work I was meant to do for the types of clients I wanted to serve.

Ultimately, this lack of consonance limited me. And as I would discover in the next stage of my career, I cared less about maximizing the bottom line and more about maximizing the impact I had on the world—while also maximizing the flexibility I wanted to retain as I grew my family and continued my community and political involvement. My new metrics of success provoked some serious side-eye from those at the best-in-the-business firm: Make enough money, but do it in a way that works for me, for my team, for our clients, and for our families.

A New Approach to Value

I still loved the work of executive search, but I felt constrained by the workplace of the traditional search firm. To position myself to explore new approaches to my industry—to change the rules of the game—I knew that I had to learn more about *why* search firms worked the way they worked. This is what I found: it was completely arbitrary.

Traditionally, executive search firms make a commission of one-third of the candidate's first year's cash compensation. So, a C-level foundation executive who was set to make $300,000 a year would generate $100,000 in commission for the search firm, while the $90,000 human services position would garner the firm only $30,000. Ipso facto, not all clients were treated or valued equally. And then there was the guarantee: If the candidate left for any reason before 365 days on the job, the firm would redo the search for free.

While there were some differences in the complexity of the work—bigger, more public positions usually demanded larger, more high-touch search committees and deeper, more extensive vetting—the higher fees weren't large enough in scale to merit such inflation. Besides, I always thought it was far easier to recruit for a fancy philanthropic position than for the scrappy domestic violence advocacy or homeless shelter human services jobs, anyway. The bigger positions paid better, had more staff and benefits, were in nicer offices in tonier neighborhoods, and came with a whole load of longer-term career value for the candidates who threw their hats into the ring.

This business model perversely incentivized many to attend more to the bigger, easier clients than to the ones who desperately needed our help and for whom the dollars spent came at a higher pain point. To make matters worse, the more work we took on, the more the firm made, so I felt pressured to take on a lot, which meant squeezing those smaller-fee searches into the last 5 percent of my time and attention most days. In short, it felt to me like the firm's outlook was *profit first, impact second*. That just wasn't in line with what had attracted me to the work in the first place: to connect qualified, mission-driven professionals with the right nonprofit job so that they could help save the world.

Our clients were all nonprofits. We all shared the same worldview, the same desire to make the world a better place. And yet, like anyone working in a job with two masters, I constantly felt that my position was to be on the other side of the table from the nonprofit client, with our firm's profit and loss statement silently plopped in between us, dividing our loyalties. We had to serve the client, but we also had to serve the firm. Our clients were fighting childhood illiteracy, cancer, and global warming—and here we were, sometimes fighting them. I wanted to be on *their* side of the table, where it was us and them against cancer. I wanted to help our clients achieve a mission we shared, using the biggest lever I had: finding them the very best talent available.

Instead, this business model pushed us to present more traditional candidates, place safer bets, and make fewer bold choices. For example, back in the late 1990s, that meant we were not pushing for as many women and people of color, because there simply weren't as many such candidates in the talent pipeline who had the twenty years of experience that presidents and CEOs were traditionally expected to have. We worried that "the first" of any kind would be rejected by a culture that didn't know how to absorb and take advantage of diversity.

I knew that the firm had never intended to end up in this position. It did have a stellar record of placing candidates who added diversity, but this was still within the bounds of carefully contained risk, of Ivy League "sure things." Perhaps none of the other employees felt the way I did, but it just didn't make sense to me. We did great work. But we did safe work. And it came at a very hefty cost to our clients when some of that money could (in my opinion) have been put to better use for their important causes. They deserved better.

I deserved better too. But it took one final straw—giving birth to my first child—to finally incentivize me to do what I did next: build a company that served both my clients and my staff (and me) equally.

Released from the grind of chasing the traditional profit and loss statement, I was able to hire nontraditional workers outside of the norm that required full-time face time. I learned to manage them based not on the time spent "in the office" but on the actual work product delivered. Starting from my living room, with a six-week-old baby by my side, I hired young mothers, international trailing spouses, part-time students, and, yes, full-time, experienced executive search consultants from my old firm, too—so many, in fact, that the president of that firm called me up one day and asked me to stop stealing his staff.

But here's the kicker: I never placed a single outgoing call to recruit from his team. They reached out to us—after we put together our own employment proposition centered around (you guessed it!) consonance.

Redefining Success

Because we knew that we wanted to maximize *impact* instead of profit, we had to run our business differently. We cut back on overhead, unpacking what it would take to deliver an exceptional search for our clients. We decided to do something radical: charge our clients not an arbitrary percentage of the salary for the position to be filled but according to the complexity of the search and the amount of work needed to get it done. Sounds like plain old common sense, right?

I gave my staff, who were hired on an hourly basis, the flexibility to do as much or as little work as they wanted and could handle, and to do that work from their home offices if they chose. This gave them control over their own earning potential and professional growth trajectory in a way that made sense for them. They were paid the same fee for each project. And the clients paid for the cost of our labor instead of cutting us commissions that went up or down based on the salary (that we negotiated) for the position we filled.

With this innovative model, we simultaneously leveled the playing field for our clients and incentivized our staff to do good work, period. That good work begat more good work, and for the first ten years our firm grew at the rate of almost 100 percent per year.

Each of us on the payroll made more money than we had made for similar work at the traditional jobs from which we defected (*contribution*). What's more, we got to work on the projects that interested us, and we worked out of the comfort of our homes, with flexibility about how much we took on and when (*control*). We got to open the curtain and show our clients how we made the magic; in the bargain, this helped them to feel comfortable making bolder choices (*connection*).

We strengthened the sector, built our reputations, and catapulted our careers further in a field that was important to us and for causes we held dear (*calling*).

I sold that company in 2016 to the team members who had helped me build it. During the fifteen years that I ran the company, I learned a great many things—both from those within my firm and from the thousands of leaders we interviewed. Chief among them was this: workers with consonance know what matters to them, and are more effective, more efficient, and more engaged for the long haul. They are limitless.

Each of us defines this differently at different times in our careers. I had to figure out what mattered to my clients. I had to figure out what mattered to my staff. I had to figure out what mattered to me.

Now it's time to figure out what matters to *you*.

Chapter 3:

Measuring What Matters

First things first—first thing in the morning, that is. Your alarm rings out, rousing you from slumber. What are your first thoughts? How do you approach the day? Do you jump up to greet it and make it count, excited to tackle the challenges ahead, to suck the marrow out of life, knowing full well how each thread of effort weaves into the larger tapestry of impact? Or do you groan, hit the snooze button, roll over, and close your eyes again, fantasizing about working basically anywhere else on earth, doing anything else on earth?

Perhaps you aren't as giddy as the eager beaver jumping out of bed. But if your demeanor is anything approaching that of the groaning, cover-burrowing wretch, you've got some work to do.

Let me be crystal clear here: There is no perfect answer. There is no perfect person. The priority you place on each of the four elements of consonance will create a combination that looks like no one else's but your own, and that's what will make it right for you. That's why it will make you limitless.

Like a DJ at a stereo mixing board, you can control the levels of each element of consonance, resulting in the sound that works for you. Hip-hop requires more bass and less treble than jazz; different kinds of music are right for different people. You need to find the right combination for who you are now and, later, for who you become as you evolve throughout your career and life. And you can't figure it out until you stop asking the jazz-lovers to rate your hip-hop performance.

Believe me, I know. Because despite the eventual success of my firm, I still had some major growing pains that were limiting me. It all started because I was using the wrong scorecard.

The Wrong Scorecard

For too long, we've measured what matters using an outdated list of universal boxes to check, one that asks us to decide our opinion of a potential job based on metrics limited by old economies and previous generations. Using metrics that measure the job before using metrics that measure *our own interests* is precisely why we burrow under the bedcovers and hit snooze. When we take only from what is offered to us, picking the best worst choice, we fail to carve a path based on what we really want. From the very start, we accept that there should be limits—and then we wonder why we find ourselves constrained by those limits.

When the company I founded was five years old, I sat down with a business coach. Things had been going well, but I knew that with the right help, we could build the company even bigger and better. Ever the gold star chaser, I brought a whole host of spreadsheets and strategic plans and marketing collateral to the meeting, looking to show off. But, much to my chagrin, the coach didn't look at a single one of my documents. Instead, he asked me one seemingly innocent question: "How do you pay yourself?"

I'm not ashamed to say that I gave him a terrible answer. I was doing the usual rookie entrepreneur thing: paying myself whatever was left over at the end of the month. I ate what I killed; some months were steak, some months were ramen. I'd pay my staff, pay my expenses, invest back into the company what was needed, conservatively sock away a little for a rainy day, and then pay myself what remained. I told all this to my coach, proud of the fact that I was doing pretty okay.

He took one look at me and told me to stop being an idiot.

Ouch.

And then he gave me some homework.

Updating the Metrics of Success

The business coach's recommendation sounded simple enough: write down a list of goals about the kind of life I wanted to live. As it turns out, this wasn't simple at all. What he wanted to hear was not just that I dreamed of having "a successful business" and "a happy home life" and "a fulfilling career." Instead, he wanted me to define what each of those things meant to me.

When I told him I wanted to travel the world, he asked how fancy the hotels would be and whether I'd be satisfied flying coach. When I told him I wanted my home life to be harmonious, he asked if that meant the flexibility to leave work when I wanted so I could attend my kids' music recitals and ultimate frisbee tournaments. When I told him I wanted a fulfilling career, he asked how I would know that I was fulfilled, and how I was defining *career*.

What the business coach was asking me to do was describe for him *why* I was doing what I was doing. He wanted me to let go of the traditional definitions of *success*. He was guiding me to figure out which boxes I really, truly wanted to check off, and not letting me be satisfied with showing off how pretty I'd made the checkmarks.

I had been thinking in the terms that are familiar to most of us throughout our working lives, the terms we use to rate the value of a job: its mission or goal; the opportunities it provides for leadership, challenge, and impact; what new skills or prestige it might bring; and the financial or other personal rewards we expect it to provide. These terms, he explained, are too general, too broad, too universal. Instead, he wanted me to figure out what job or work scenario would produce the right balance *for me* of the metrics that mattered *to me*.

Though I didn't realize it yet, what he was asking me to do was translate the potential value of the job not just as the marketplace would rate it, but measured against my own personal needs—the metrics which I would later distill into "the four elements of consonance": *calling, connection, contribution,* and *control.*

The exercise helped me realize that I needed to figure out how to save the world through my lever of talent (*I care!*), while also building a business that would throw off enough income to afford first-class travel (*But I'm also a princess!*). How could I check off both boxes when each demanded full commitment—when each opposing set of goals was filled with judgment about my activities in pursuit of the other? I didn't think I could.

Forced to answer these questions, however, I discovered that I was going through the motions with my business, hurtling forward with momentum and goals, but no specific purpose. I had *connection* with how my work was building the company I'd started. I had *control* over whom we hired and which clients were part of our portfolio. I enjoyed getting deep into the muck and solving problems in partnership with our clients, all of which were nonprofits, allowing me to wear the white hat while helping save the world, even if it didn't quite yet afford me the first-class airline seats. But I was still behaving like a hamster on a wheel, just running faster and faster, trying to serve more clients and manage more staff.

My company continued to grow by leaps and bounds, but our profit margin only took baby steps. My frustration was increasing. We were working harder, but not scaling our income along with our impact. I was limited by that old scorecard. When I tried to solve the problem, I kept coming back to the on-paper version of success that told me I was getting it all right. I couldn't find the solution because I couldn't see the real problem.

It wasn't until I stopped to consider the *contribution* that I wanted this work to make to the life I wanted to live—more flexibility to be involved in my community and family, more money for those fancy airline seats, and more of a way to live the values that I held dear about the world I wanted to create—that I was able to build the company in a way that completed my picture of purpose.

For me, this meant no longer trying to be all things to all people, so I brought on a business partner who could do the internal management and develop the team—not my strong suit. That freed me to be the out-front champion of our people and the proselytizer about our bold new way of doing search, which is where I was at my best and where I had the most fun. Once I learned to interpret the old way of measuring the value of a job through the new way of determining what gave me consonance, I eschewed the limits that constrained me. And when I did, we thrived.

Rehabilitating the Eight Motivating Factors

Back in high school and college, guidance counselors were there to help you plot out a future educational path based on the career choices that were expected of you by parents, teachers, friends, and potential employers. You studied your options and then you placed a value on each job opportunity, choosing from a scorecard of checkboxes that were meant to guide you.

But in the end, those checkboxes were only limiting you.

These metrics probably included the following eight motivating factors that were intended to help you rate the specific value of your first job. And, whether you knew it or not, these eight metrics probably influenced your thinking about every job you've taken since.

- *Mission*: What is the goal of the organization, department, or job? Do you have passion for the work of the company or cause? Does it matter to you personally?

- *Leadership*: Are you iknspired by those in charge? Are you encouraged, motivated, and cheered on by those at the top? Do you respect and look forward to being taught by the leadership of the company?

- *Challenge*: Is the work in question something that interests you? Do you feel as though the job represents something bigger than just you? Does it force you to dig in and be your best self?

- *Scope of impact*: Does your work matter? Will it make a difference? How much, how broad, and how deep will the scope of your impact be?

- *Acquisition of new skills*: Do you need to up your game in order to be successful in this job? Will you learn new skills? Will those skills directly benefit the future you?

- *Prestige*: Is the reputation of the company or brand something you can be proud of? Are you happy to talk about your work in public and to family and friends? Does the job make you feel good? Will it look good on your resume?

- *Personal needs*: Does the job allow you to make accommodations for additional concerns in your life, such as ailing parents or small children? Do you have a side gig that forces distinct scheduling needs, such as consulting or teaching, a beloved hobby, a custody arrangement, or an impairment or personal obstacle? Are you seeking employment that offers flexibility, benefits, or geographical considerations that differ from the norm?

- *Money*: And then, of course, there is money. For some, it's the number one issue. For many, however, it takes a back seat to other priorities. How much do you need to make? How much do you want to make?

Now, don't get me wrong. These eight metrics are useful. But they provide an incomplete picture. They are floating in space, untethered to what matters to *you*.

The truth is, everyone looks at these metrics differently.

For some, on the upswing of their career, the brand prestige, the acquisition of new skills, and the scope of impact will matter more than the mission or the money. For others, perhaps balancing family demands, money, and personal needs such as flexibility will be paramount. In every case, these metrics still matter. They just don't give the full picture. And when we use them and only them, we mistake filling in checkboxes for flinging away our limits.

Take, for example, the metric of money. What you *need* to make and what you *want* to make are two different numbers. You must meet the first number; making enough money to survive is table stakes for everyone. But you can weigh the value of the other seven motivating factors as you reach for—or compromise on—the second number. Rather than thinking about these metrics to measure the job (*What does it pay?*), you should use metrics that measure yourself and your unique desires (*What kind of lifestyle do I want to live?*). By tweaking the outdated metric, you can determine how this particular work contributes to your personal definition of success.

Now let's think about a different metric that might be important to you: the prestige or brand value of the company. This involves how the company name will look on your résumé—what it will say about you and the type of person you are, what it will communicate about the training you've received or the accountability to which you've been held. Depending on your industry or field, working for a particular company certainly might have a great impact on your future career trajectory. In other words, taking a lesser job at a company that is at the top of its field could contribute greater brand value to your future career than taking a high-level job at a company with a soiled reputation. If this matters to you, then you should hold the prestige metric paramount over the others.

Thinking about these eight motivating factors is an exercise that can help you rank the metrics that matter to you. Your answers will reflect where you are at your particular age and stage of life. And here's the great news: there is no wrong answer.

Discovering a Deeper Need

If you're shaking your head, realizing that you have been thinking far too narrowly about your career for far too long, don't feel bad. Given my career as an executive recruiter, I'm supposedly the expert, and it took me some time to figure it out, too.

As I was smiling and dialing, cold calling candidates and recruiting them out of the blue, I relied on the old scorecard of those eight motivating factors—mission, leadership, challenge, scope of impact, acquisition of new skills, prestige, personal needs, and money—as signposts along a roadmap: If I heard interest in one or two of those metrics, I knew there would be a second conversation. If I heard interest in three or four, I knew the bait was on the hook. And any more than five nibbles meant that the candidate was practically in the boat.

Once I knew what to listen for, building the candidate pools was like shooting fish in a barrel. But then I noticed something else happening: my candidate pools, though rich in numbers and potential, would slowly disintegrate as the three- to four-month search process dragged on. A once-robust pool would dwindle as my prospects dropped out of the search, one by one, for a variety of reasons. These motivating factors all remained important considerations—try as I might, I've never been able to get my bank to take good karma in exchange for a mortgage payment. But what mattered more than the amount of money offered was *what the money meant to the candidate and the life he or she was building.*

Until I was able to figure out the true value of the money, the leadership, the mission, and so forth—that is, the value assigned by that candidate in particular—I was simply checking boxes. And that didn't stick.

You see, I was trying to sell a product—the job—to people who weren't necessarily in the market. I was calling them because they were successful at what they were doing and because that success made them attractive to my client, the employer. I was asking them to throw their hat into the ring for a search they didn't even know existed until they picked up the phone. And rather than a value proposition that was meaningful to the person on the other end of the line, I was armed only with generic checkboxes.

Once I realized this, I knew that the only way to nestle into the imagination of a candidate and inspire them, to really influence them to care about the potential new position, was to make the correlation to a deeper need. I had to show them that they were limited by the way they currently interpreted those metrics. Then they could see themselves, in the job I was offering, as limitless.

The job I was offering wasn't simply about the money, the brand prestige, or the acquisition of new skills. It was about how the income could contribute to the life that person wanted to live, how the value of the brand could contribute to his or her career development, and how the bigger toolkit acquired in this new position would help them bring velocity to their chosen trajectory. So, to speak to the values and needs of the individual candidate for a particular job, I had to go deeper.

But that wasn't all. Depending on the individual, I could then take each of those eight factors—each of the person's treasured values I had dug down deep to uncover—and broaden these into a larger conversation about consonance. For the people who valued *connection*, I could talk about the advantages offered by the company's strong leadership or the challenges the job represented. For those who needed a deeper sense of *calling*, I went straight to the firm's innovative mission or the wide-ranging impact that came with the position. I could discuss *contribution* not just through the salary and benefits package, but also through the values that the company manifested in its work. And I could talk about *control* by telling stories of other workers who had sought and achieved similar promotions, flexibility, or agency.

My business coach was right. Finding the right work isn't about checking off the boxes on a list of timeworn values, metrics, and choices. It's about how this list gives us a way to measure consonance, to understand whether the work we do matters to us. It's about using this list to remove the limits placed on us by someone else's expectations.

Once I understood this, my close rate went way up. Candidates had a reason to be in the hunt for work that mattered to them. They had a reason to stick it out through the long and demanding search process. They could see how this product I was peddling—the job—was in consonance with their own life plan. They could feel the limits being lifted off them as they imagined themselves in the potential role. It just made sense.

And once you understand what these metrics mean to you—what they mean *for* you—it will begin to make sense for you, too.

PART TWO

THE FOUR ELEMENTS
OF CONSONANCE

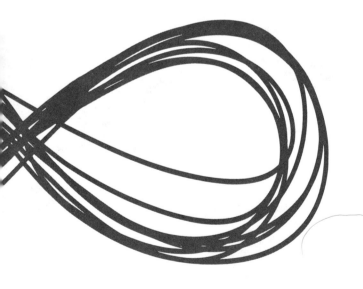

Chapter 4

Calling

As a college student at an Episcopal university, Lonsdale Koester thought she had a calling to become a priest. Family, faculty, and friends were all supportive and encouraging, but along her path to her future career she faced roadblock after roadblock, from outdated thinking to church bureaucracy. A few years later, she was working a nonprofit job in Washington, DC and still stubbornly trying to enter the ordination process. One day, a lay member of her church's governing body took her to lunch at a Tex-Mex restaurant and said words she'd never forget: "You don't have to be a priest to be a minister."

This moment was mind-blowing, trajectory-changing, life-affirming—and probably the first and only sober epiphany ever experienced at the Cactus Cantina.

Instead of following the calling into the church, Lonsdale followed her secular calling to make a difference in the world and pursued a master's degree in public policy, focused on performance management. At the time, George W. Bush was in the White House, and despite the fact that she disagreed with most of his Republican policies, Lonsdale was attracted to the office of faith-based initiatives that President Bush supported. She wanted to learn more about the positive impact that could be had through alliances between religious organizations and the government.

After graduation, Lonsdale began volunteering and raising money for the campaign of Deval Patrick, a Democrat outsider running for governor of Massachusetts. Her heart was drawn to his personal story and his passion for creating equity of opportunity for all people, especially those on the margins. Her head was drawn to the way in which Patrick surrounded himself with people who were open to discovery, who were curious, who were interested in learning new things. She found herself in the scrum of the campaign and later, after Patrick won, serving in his administration, where she eventually ran a performance management system for the state.

Politics and public policy might be a far cry from the priesthood, but, viewed through the lens of making a difference in the world and living out her values, Lonsdale unquestionably found her calling.

What Is Calling?

The most obvious and most frequent use of the term *calling* is in the traditional religious, nonprofit, or cause-driven way. It's true that working for a cause that is bigger than ourselves can bring great meaning to our work. We feel good about ourselves when we are doing things for others, and regardless of whether that cause is intimate (such as helping those in your very own community) or anonymous (such as funding vaccinations in third-world countries), it comes with karmic reward. Knowing that you are part and parcel of making the world a better place can be a vital piece of your calling.

Yet this is just one of many interpretations of calling. Cause doesn't have to be part of the equation for everyone. In fact, for some people it can even be detrimental to the pursuit of purpose, because the sacrifices they make in order to serve—their willingness to accept a lower salary, fewer benefits, and less flexibility—make them less connected, less contributory, less in control than they would otherwise be. You can fight like hell for your cause all day long, but sometimes it still feels like just a drop in the bucket. Limiting your concept of calling to the religious or charitable sense of the word can be damned frustrating, to say the least.

This may seem ironic, given that I've spent my career in service to the nonprofit world, encouraging people to upend their careers and join the ranks. Nevertheless, I consider this narrow interpretation of calling to be problematic. Not only is it incomplete, but it also prevents people from looking for consonance at every stage in their careers. Instead, they assume that following their calling simply isn't for them—or at least, not until some later date when they retire.

Ask yourself: why does your calling have to be a higher calling? Why can't it simply be the overarching thing that guides the decisions you make about your career? Can't you have purpose if you are building a company, building a community, building a family? Isn't that enough?

A Limited Definition of Calling

Remember that executive search firm that I founded and ran for fifteen years? Yes, it served the nonprofit sector, but the firm itself was decidedly for-profit. Long before the rise in popularity of socially responsible businesses or the advent of B Corps (companies that balance profit and purpose), our purpose-driven business model left loads of money on the table by focusing first and foremost on living our values and creating an employment proposition equal to our client proposition. Yet we still made a hefty profit because our business model was so innovative and efficient. I liked to call us not a "for-profit" company, but a "for-enough-profit" company: cause-driven, but still profit-focused.

I point out the difference because it flies in the face of an assumption many of us hold: that purpose comes only from wearing the white hat, from noble nonprofit work, from the land of service and sacrifice. And this simply isn't true for everyone. Purpose for me was, in fact, that higher calling to serve, but I didn't become limitless until I figured out how that life of service fit into the other 148 hours per week when I wasn't in the office.

In order to understand why we cling to that mistaken assumption, it's important to learn where it comes from in the first place. And that place is Plymouth Rock.

Mistaking Charity for Purpose

The Pilgrims were Puritans, Calvinists through and through. Persecuted for practicing their religion and seeking to earn enough money to live comfortably, they left England in pursuit of the freedom to do both. They found half of this equation—religious freedom—in Holland, but without the ability to make money, they decided to move on.

The problem with being a Calvinist, however, is that earning any more money than you need to live a puritanical life comes with pesky puritanical guilt. So if you are good at making money, you need to figure out what to do about the guilt that comes with it. And this is where John Winthrop comes into the story.

On the ships from Europe to North America—the very ships that carried hopes and dreams of better and (ahem!) more purposeful lives—John Winthrop gave a sermon about charity, calling it the truest form of salvation. And here's the rub: Charity didn't save the poor, as we like to imagine it today. It was salvation for the guilty, for the rich. Charity was the penance that the Puritans paid for making money.

Guilt, it turns out, was good for business. Those same Puritans elected Winthrop the governor of the Massachusetts Bay Colony several times over, further enshrining his words into law. And that shining "city upon a hill" he sermonized about? This idea is at the root of the nonprofit sector in the United States today.

In fact, the entire nonprofit sector formed around the assumption that it is the responsibility of those with more to take care of those with less. It is a wonderful concept based on empathy, compassion, grace, and, yes, charity. But it has also conditioned us to think and work in the wrong way, by presuming that one's calling can be worthy only by having its foundation in some charitable purpose.

Service Doesn't Have to Be Sacrifice

From its religious roots, this notion of charity led to the creation of nonprofits that were tasked with organizing and facilitating the delivery of a wide range of services to the poor, needy, and underserved. Fast-forward several hundred years to the vastly expanded nonprofit sector today in the United States,[11] where charity has gone from being a form of salvation to populating a series of ledger lines— profit and loss statements that, at the end of the day, have to show no profit. The founding of our charitable impulses, based on heart-strings rather than economics, has transformed into big business. But it has retained multiple masters.

Imagine you run a nonprofit that helps under-served children. Most of your money comes in the form of donations from individuals, foundations, or government grants. Who are your customers: the children or the donors? You'd like to think you serve the children, but this is not the case. The children are merely the beneficiaries. Your donors—the people you need to keep happy because they provide the revenue that keeps you afloat—are your true customers. This creates a major problem that continues to hamstring the nonprofit sector.

As the sector grew, and continued its attempts to keep well-meaning (but misinformed) donors happy, nonprofits were forced to

---

11 The nonprofit sector is made up of 1.57 million organizations and pays 9.2 percent of all wages in the United States, not including the many religious organizations that, ironically, are exempted from registering as nonprofits. "Quick Facts about Nonprofits," National Center for Charitable Statistics, accessed October 2, 2018, https://tinyurl.com/yapqj58u.

answer questions about the *cost* of delivering programs rather than the *effectiveness* of those programs. Overhead concerns dictated lower investments in staff, research and development, and program evaluation. Nonprofit work became synonymous with constant cost-cutting and martyrdom, taking on the role of "the sector of good" and "the true path to purpose," where sacrifice was praised in benefactors but downright expected of staff members.

The nonprofit sector has thus unintentionally shaped our idea of purpose, asserting that we can't have purpose if we aren't of service—and that we can't be of service if we aren't experiencing sacrifice.

Getting Siloed

Chalk one up for your hatred of taxes, because it turns out that they are partly to blame for our frustrations. Our universe of employment options is siloed, first and foremost, into nonprofit and for-profit options. Beneath each of those are the various industries: government, academia, philanthropy, advocacy, human services, military, and so forth. Or, if you prefer, consider the silos as privately held companies, publicly held companies, and a whole host of small business and entrepreneurial endeavors. Any way you look at it, there's a predetermined diagram that defines how we are boxed—and how we box ourselves.

The assumption that purpose is a function of charity and sacrifice has also created an environment where nonprofits historically grew as essentially volunteer entities while corporations became the platform for "real" careers. But the nonprofit sector was not to be contained, evolving fast and furiously, from turn-of-the-century settlement houses that focused on child welfare ... to advocacy around labor laws and organizing for women's suffrage ... to the Great Depression, when it acted as a social safety net ... to the massive cultural shift brought about by the civil rights era, the environmental movement, and the Vietnam War, inspiring citizens to act collectively to bring about faster and greater impact. With this growth came demands for more professionalization, but because most of the nonprofit staff's attention was focused primarily on service delivery, serious training for real careers in the sector lagged behind. Senior leadership positions were filled by former field and program staff for whom management and professional development was forced to be an afterthought.

Our institutions of higher education had to play catch-up once the sector began to demand more training, more education, and more certification. Their reaction was to create bespoke nonprofit management courses, and this has worked out well for those seeking to be trained for a career in the nonprofit sector. Thirty years ago, only a few universities offered graduate degrees in nonprofit management, but there are now more than two hundred. Graduates now come to the sector better prepared than ever, and the results that nonprofits have in bringing about change are remarkable.

But this trend has made life harder for people whose calling shifts as they pass through various stages of life. Because of the grooved patterns of the "tax-code silo" mindset, students are still being trained for one sector or the other. Workers can find it challenging to transition fluidly between the sectors later in their careers, despite the fact that so many of the skills developed in one silo would benefit and transfer to the other. The end result is a pair of incorrect notions: First, that purpose is "over there" for "people in those jobs" in "that sector." And second, that true meaning and purpose are unachievable in the career we may have already chosen.

*　*　*　*　*

So, if calling isn't charity ... if it isn't sacrifice ... if it isn't limited to nonprofit work ... then what is it?

Bottom line: your calling is whatever you need it to be. It is your raison d'être, your very own compass pointing towards consonance. It is your personal motivation, the purpose behind it all, the reason you jump out of bed in the morning. Your calling allows you to identify how you make an impact and bring value—it's a constant reminder of what matters. And whether it's a charitable cause, an entrepreneurial drive, or something else, no one gets a vote in what matters—except you.

Four Ways to Bring Calling to Your Work

Rick Muhr lives and breathes running. He oozes confidence, competence, and compassion in the way that all great coaches do. He loves the sport, but even more than that, he loves coaching the sport. An avid runner since his Air Force days, Rick started coaching when he saw a sign for the Leukemia & Lymphoma Society charity runners' program during a marathon. He knew immediately that training their runners would be the perfect way to honor his mother, who had died of leukemia.

After making inroads into the coaching community, in 2008 Rick helped cofound the Marathon Coalition, a nonprofit through which he has trained hundreds of charity runners (including me!) to complete the Boston Marathon and raise over $2 million annually. Although he earned a small income through the Marathon Coalition, he was still paying the bills by managing nationwide teams of salespeople at Pearson Education, and later for Polo Ralph Lauren, in jobs that had called to him at first. He believed in the brands, saw how his work influenced the bottom line, knew how it contributed to the life he wanted to live, and felt control over how much his hustle would affect his income and career growth.

Yet as Rick became increasingly disillusioned with the pursuit of grinding out quarterly sales goals, he realized that the calling he felt wasn't deep enough. He wanted to make running his full-time life. But he couldn't see how to scale the Marathon Coalition to a size that would pay him enough to walk away from his lucrative national sales jobs.

In 2013, while walking through the Boston Marathon Expo—an enormous pre-race fair where businesses that cater to runners gather to hock wares like GPS watches, heart rate monitors, athletic clothing, nutritional supplements, sneakers, and fitness equipment—Rick noticed something he hadn't seen before: a completely zero-impact running machine. The Zero Runner, made by Octane Fitness, promised long-distance runners the holy grail: being able to run forever and ever, with no harm to their joints. As Rick struck up a conversation with the founders, he learned something that would change his life: The founders were having trouble getting traction and needed help with a national sales strategy and execution. And Rick knew just the guy for the job.

If you're looking for Rick now, you can find him traveling the country, getting paid to talk to runners, all day long, about running. That is, until he gets home and talks to Marathon Coalition runners, all weekend long, about running.

So, how can you find your calling, as Rick found his? And how will you incorporate it into your life's plan?

Find What Fuels You

Calling is your own personal higher purpose. It can be an overarching motivation, a goal to reach, a problem to solve, a societal ill to remedy, or a worthwhile cause to serve. It can be a bottom line to meet, a business to build, a brand to love. It's the direction of an overall goal and the particular pride you attach to the value of that goal.

Your calling can be found in the shape of a cause that you want to help for a nonprofit you'd like to serve. But it can also be corporate work. Employees who feel good about the overall mission of their place of work can feel equally good about that work whether it is Special Olympics or Procter & Gamble or, in Rick's case, Octane Fitness. What matters is that the calling, the brand, the bigger thing to which you are attached has meaning to you. It is your why.

And yes, if you are an entrepreneur, you can be your own calling. Nothing provides clarity about your calling more than your own motivation driving you to achieve your dream. History is filled with successful entrepreneurs—think Henry Ford, Oprah Winfrey, Steve Jobs, Madonna—who never wavered in their focus on who they were and what they wanted out of their fleeting time on this earth.

In the aftermath of the 1986 IPO that would make Bill Gates a billionaire, his mother urged him to give some of his money away. He reportedly told her that he was too busy running his company and didn't want to be limited by those distractions just yet. Some saw this as a selfish act and took a wait-and-see approach about whether or not he really would be philanthropic later.

But, like all of us, Gates worked best when he worked in consonance. When he was curious about coding and enjoying the challenges of problem solving, he built his company. It was what he did best, and it was his calling. Later, as he began to learn more about the causes (and effects) of extreme poverty, he dedicated $100 million to start the Bill & Melinda Gates Foundation. But it was not until he left Microsoft that his calling shifted and his work as a full-time philanthropist really took shape. Now, he has dedicated not just hundreds of millions, but billions of dollars to solve the worldwide problems of poverty, hunger, illness, and inequality at their roots.

If you are unsure about your calling, ask yourself: what fuels me? The answer should help to clarify your purpose and bring it into greater alignment with your working life.

Make Deposits in the Future Bank of You

Do what you love and you'll never have to work a day in your life. It's decent advice but, once again, incomplete.

Figuring out what you love to do is a good thing. But making that one thing define your entire career is not. As you grow and evolve throughout your life, as you master tasks and solve puzzles, you will naturally seek out new challenges. Having the guts to confront those challenges is part of investing in your passion. If you hold too tightly to one identity, the uncertainty of losing it—who am I if not an accountant (or lawyer, or teacher, or bricklayer)?—can be so unsettling that career recalibration feels overwhelming.

Plus, resting a career on a first love will become boring. The part of consonance that comes from acquiring new skills and being challenged will drop from the equation. Instead, think about what you love to do with a more aspirational mindset. That is, think about what you'd like to love to do in the future, not just what you have loved to do in the past.

Don't be afraid of that divergence. Though it can be disconcerting, I've always been attracted to positions for which I have no seemingly obvious qualifications. The space in between *what you are qualified to do* and *what you want to do* is the credit advance you get on that passion investment; it is the nest egg of the skills and network and knowledge you'll need to acquire. And these are all deposits in the Future Bank of You.

Take an Attention Inventory

As you think about what you are qualified to do, don't just stop at the borders of your paid work. This is where many fail in their quest to turn their work into their calling. They rely solely on how others have defined them in terms of their day jobs, and forget to look at the broader picture of the skills and competencies on which they have focused their attention.

You have probably gathered skills at work that are readily inventoried. But what about the rest of the hours in your day? What have you done for your child's school? How have you volunteered in your place of worship? What have you learned along the way through your involvement in neighborhood committees? Have your hobbies or leisure activities lent you expertise relevant to your new career path?

Better still, what have you done in your workplace that is outside of your regular job? Perhaps it's something you think doesn't belong on your résumé because it's not in your job description. Or maybe it's an aptitude or proficiency that feels like ancient history to you because it's from several jobs back. Why aren't you boasting about these skills that you still have in spades?

Taking an attention inventory benefits you in two ways. First, and most obviously, this exercise gives you a sense of the skills you bring to bear as you consider making the changes necessary to find your calling. Less obviously, however, it helps you understand where you have put your attention. What we pay attention to is what grows. So, a good indication of what you care about—what you are willing to work for, what might be your calling—is to figure out where you've spent your time and energy. Or where you wish you had.

Tend Your Crops

Maybe you're thinking, *it's all well and good for her to tell me to go out and find my calling, but this privilege isn't available to me*—at least, not immediately. There are bills to pay, children to raise, classes to take. Whatever "it" is, it's getting in your way. Dreaming gets back-burnered, vision-boarded, bucket-listed. But there are things you can and should do today—right now!—to start the process of figuring out your calling, and they all involve increasing your optionality.

Put another way, these are classic video-game side quests. Just ask my teenage son, who first introduced me to this concept one morning when I was moaning about being stuck and unable to move forward on a project.

"Mom," he so very patiently explained, "it's like when you need to go slay the dragon so you can save the princess in the castle, but first you have to wait for your friends to finish their family dinner so they can log on and play with you. You can't move forward without them. So while you wait, you can go tend your crops so you have wheat to sell at the market that you pass along the way to the castle. And when you sell the wheat, you can buy a new horse or a fancy sword that you know you'll need later when you come upon that dragon."

Side quests are related to your larger goal, but not on the direct path. Allow yourself to reframe your current problem as an opportunity to increase your future optionality by collecting people, knowledge, networks, and resources that you will need later. Say yes to the networking event. Talk to strangers. Take a class. Ask to tag along to a presentation. You never know who you might meet, what you might learn, where your interests will pull you, or what dragons you'll slay.

Questions to Guide Your Search for Calling

Finding your calling and becoming limitless often require that you follow a nontraditional, nonlinear path. Some people get to that point in their journey through planned strategic action; others look back and pat themselves on the back for having been there all along. Regardless, your calling comes not from a career manual, but from the heart. Your calling is as you, and only you, define it.

Dropping out of a Wall Street lifestyle to move to Cambodia and build wells won't make you an anomaly any more than getting certified as a yoga teacher and working part time when your kids go to school. Don't shy away from something that might seem far out. In twenty years of interviewing candidates, I've found that those with the most nonlinear paths offer the most interesting insights, having gathered unique perspective and wisdom along the way. Keep an open mind, think broadly, and adapt your search for professional meaning accordingly.

Each of us can and should be the entrepreneurial force in our own life, understanding and owning our calling and letting it drive our professional path toward becoming limitless. That insatiable goal—whether it's feeding the poor, making your company shine, or going after that lofty promotion—that's your calling.

As you figure out your calling, consider the following questions:

- Can you identify your overarching goal?
- Does your work bring about the change you want to make in your company, your community, your country, your world?
- Would you work harder or keep longer hours if what you did mattered to you more?
- What do you enjoy more: your volunteer work or your regular job? Why?
- Do you feel proud of the mission of your employer?
- Why do you do the work that you do?

Chapter 5

Connection

Scott Monty spent the early part of his career working in a variety of communications roles on behalf of both corporate and nonprofit entities—sometimes in-house, sometimes as a consultant. Then one day he landed his dream job as global digital and multimedia communications manager for Ford Motor Company. At the time, dynamic and visionary CEO Alan Mulally was dragging the company and the entire auto industry into a new era, and Scott was reporting directly to the head of communications, who was reporting directly to Alan.

From the mission of the company, the leadership of the company, the direction of the company—Scott felt a calling. He saw clearly how the work he did connected to the bottom line of a Fortune 10 company and the ripple effects that it had in the industry and the corporate sector as a whole.

But then Mulally announced he would be leaving, and the company started to shift back to its old bureaucratic ways. Scott's connection to the work became murky, and his efficacy was dulled. While he was still busy, he could no longer connect his work to the impact it should have. His role as the strategic lead of digital was significantly discounted, and that shook his confidence.

Scott had given all of himself to Ford, with the hours he was working quickly superseding the commitments he'd made to his wife and young children. Scott was stuck in a grind of work that didn't feel important, with people whom he didn't like, in an environment that didn't value what he loved to do and excelled at doing. He had not only lost connection to his work; he was not connected at home, either. So he left his job.

Scott started Brain+Trust Partners, and now works with industry leaders as a consigliere of sorts, helping to break up inertia and provide bottom-line building insights and recommendations based on his breadth of experience. Plus, as a keynote speaker, he shows audiences how to focus relentlessly on the customer. He has replicated what gave him his calling at Ford, but broadened it to serve even more groundbreaking companies. Now Scott can see a direct connection between his work and the companies that his clients are trying to grow—and he's able to spend more time at home with his family, too.

What Is Connection?

What if you didn't show up to work tomorrow? Would it matter?

Not all of us have that satisfying sense that the tasks we perform on a daily basis connect to the cause we want to serve, the problem we want to solve, the company we want to build. It's why we don't feel guilty about calling in sick or punching out a little early to beat traffic. It's also why we aren't shocked to hear that American workers feel less and less engaged in their jobs every year.[12] Yet each of us, in each job we fill, *is* part of something larger: a box on an organizational chart that has local, regional, and perhaps even national and global goals. So the work you do might very well matter; perhaps you just don't have the sightlines that allow you to visualize the connection.

---

12 Gallup polls consistently find that only one-third of US workers feel actively engaged in their jobs. Amy Adkins, "Employee Engagement in U.S. Stagnant in 2015," *Workplace* (blog), Gallup.com, January 13, 2016, https://tinyurl.com/ydagwkhf.

As slaves to the Tyranny of Urgency, we get distracted and mistake being busy and stressed for doing important work. We run on the hamster wheel, doing more work, but not necessarily work that matters. Don't believe me? Try to describe your biggest professional achievements this year, the ones of which you are most proud.

No, wait. Start again.

You probably started by using the word *we*, as in *we achieved this* or *we succeeded at that*. For the purposes of this exercise, however, I want you to ignore the manners your mama taught you and be horrifyingly self-centered. (Don't worry, I won't tell. Pinky promise!)

Start again, using the word *I*, and answer the following questions: What goals would never have been accomplished but for the fact that you, specifically you, were in that job? Can you draw a clear, distinct line from your daily work to your monthly, quarterly, or yearly goals? And how does that work impact the calling you wish to serve?

If you can't answer these questions, you probably don't have—or at least don't feel as though you have—connection. And without understanding how your work connects to that calling you hold dear, you will be frustrated. Becoming limitless demands connection.

A Lack of Perspective

Why do we keep running on that hamster wheel, working harder and harder but not feeling like we are making progress? Why do we put our nose to the grindstone in pursuit of completing our to-do list or emptying our inbox when those things have nothing to do with the larger strategic imperatives weighing down on us? Why do we keep acting when our actions are so obviously not connected to fulfilling our calling?

It all starts with a lack of perspective on the actual problem we are trying to solve. And we gain perspective only when we step back and reevaluate how we connect with—and through—our work.

Action Doesn't Equal Impact

When a gunman killed twenty children and six adults at Sandy Hook Elementary School, more than sixty-seven thousand teddy bears descended on Newtown, Connecticut. And that's just a fraction of what showed up after Hurricane Sandy in New York and New Jersey, Super Typhoon Haiyan in the Philippines, and the Japanese earthquake that caused the Fukushima disaster. Have you ever wondered what happens to all these teddy bears? Some end up in the hands of small children, like the little rays of hope that they were intended to be. But by far the vast majority end up piled in dumpsters, waiting to be incinerated.

Now, it feels good—to us—to send teddy bears. The desire to comfort comes from the best part of our humanity, and it is a noble impulse. Of course, there is nothing wrong with wanting to send a teddy bear to a struggling child, just like there is nothing wrong with wanting to fund a bed in a homeless shelter during a blizzard, or give a pint of blood after a terrorist attack. These efforts do good, and they create a feeling of connection to the cause.

But that connection is only temporary.

As good as they feel, as noble as they are, these efforts don't solve the problem. We allow ourselves to be heartened in the cathedrals of short-term comfort, of doing *something*, when really we need to be building institutions of long-term change—of doing the *right thing*. Fast-forward to the next disaster, the next attack, the next shocking news story, and we feel stymied. That delicate, cotton-candy sense of connection—that momentary dopamine hit, that ego-boosting pat on the back—disappears quickly. We're left grappling with the same questions: *Why did it happen again? What can I do to help? How can I do something that actually matters?*

Too often, we decide how to act based on our limited, short-term perspective of what is needed in order to solve a given situation. When we fail to take a long-term view, our quick fixes don't contribute to the world we want to create. When we fail to envision the right solution, we're unable to align our acts with how we might leverage our best skills. Sure, we had action—but we didn't have impact. Without impact, we don't have a lasting connection to how those actions actually make a difference, actually matter.

And we wonder why we feel so limited in our ability to get anything done.

Asking the Right Question

This contrast—the exhaustion from being so busy versus the lack of progress we are actually making—shows up again and again in the conversations I've had with hundreds of leaders over the course of my career. The ones who focused on the daily tasks (the action) felt overscheduled and stressed. So many felt unfulfilled, because the root-cause problem never went away. On the contrary, the ones who focused on the results (the impact) felt consonance because they could see the connection between their work and the long-term problems they were trying to solve.

What is the difference between the two? It comes down to asking the right question based on the right perspective.

Those people who choose work based on a question focusing on the short-term action—*how can I help?*—solve only short-term problems. Now, before you throw tomatoes at me, hear this: solving short-term problems is important work, and it should be attended to. Obviously, the short-term problems still need to be solved, and that activity can create connection for some. Yet most of us are stuck, frustrated, and limited until we also eventually connect that work to the long-term solution. And in my experience, those who focus on the long-term solutions, and who feel more consonance (and less burnout) over time, are asking a different question: *What needs to happen?*

Put plainly, commonsense gun control is a better solution than teddy bears.

Four Ways to Bring Connection to Your Work

Adam Foss went to law school so that he could make money, period. He had no interest in being a public servant, had no interest in criminal law, and definitely never thought he would be a prosecutor. At the end of his first year of law school, Adam got an internship in a local municipal court in a neighborhood plagued by gun violence and drug crime. His perspective was radically reframed on the very first day.

Over and over again, Adam saw judges, defense attorneys, and prosecutors making life-altering decisions about defendants without much, if any, input from the defendants themselves. His calling suddenly changed: from making money for himself to ensuring justice for all. Committed to doing better, he became a public prosecutor and connected his daily work on behalf of his clients with that end goal. He found consonance in this—or so he thought.

Then Adam met Christopher, an eighteen-year-old African American high school senior, who had his sights set on college but had precious little income to pay his way. In desperation, Christopher made a poor decision: He stole thirty laptops and tried to sell them on the internet. When it came time for Christopher's arraignment, Adam realized that he would have to make a decision that would forever affect Christopher: bring the case to trial and send the young man to jail, or leverage him into a plea deal, affording him the chance of a normal life.

Spoiler alert: Adam did the latter. With input from Christopher, they recovered 75 percent of the computers, gave them back to Best Buy, and set up a plan for financial repayment and community service. Christopher applied to college, got financial aid, graduated from a four-year school, and is now a manager at a local bank.

Adam thought that he already had a deep connection to his work, but handling Christopher's case made him realize something. While he was able to influence the outcomes for individual clients and individual cases, his daily work didn't go far enough to answer his calling:

equal justice and fairness for all. What about all the other prosecutors out there—untrained, unfettered, and unaware? They—not judges, not politicians, not sheriffs—are the ones who make the recommendations, who are the linchpin in deciding the fate of most of those arrested in the United States. Adam was just nicking around the edges, one case at a time, putting his thumb in the dike. He wasn't truly connected.

So he got strategic, using his skills as an attorney to research, argue, teach, and ultimately make the case for prosecutors to better understand and execute the powers they are given. He used his charisma, his knowledge, and his own life story; if you think I'm making that up, watch his TED talk and see. And he started Prosecutor Impact, which trains prosecutors to improve community safety through a better understanding of what he considers to be the most important actor in the criminal justice system: the prosecutor.

How can you make the necessary changes, as Adam did, to increase your understanding of how your work can be in service to your calling? How can you increase your connection so you can increase the consonance in your life?

Say Yes Better

The toughest piece of personal and career advice I've ever gotten is this: "You're just not that important." At the time, I was simultaneously building my business, building my family, and building my community, all while being all things to all people at all times. It sure *seemed* like I was important to the world around me. I was firing on all cylinders. I was kicking ass and taking names. I was leaning in. And I was killing myself trying to do it all.

This state of affairs was untenable. I had to learn how to say no. But I loved saying yes! You can't increase your optionality without saying yes. The trouble was, I thought everything I was doing was connecting to my calling, and I wanted to justify my actions.

As I sought out advice confirming that I was, in fact, a dynamo who could say yes to the whole lot, all I could find were blogs about saying no: how to say no (stall, deflect, demure), and why saying no is good for you (more time, better boundaries, bubblier baths). But nothing really talked about what to say no to.

So, rather than learning how to say no, I taught myself how to say yes better. Once I started saying yes to the right things, I no longer had time for the wrong things. It was magic! And it all came down to asking four simple questions.

First, will doing this thing help you? Make sure that you can see yourself—on the other side of this project, promotion, bake sale, committee chairmanship, or [insert sucker-punch-of-an-ask here]—getting closer to achieving your set of personal or professional goals.

Second, will doing this thing help someone else? While some requests may appear to pay you in nothing more than psychic karma, perhaps they come with a useful side dish: bringing you to new places, introducing you to new people, teaching you about new topics, or handing you new skills.

Third, will doing this thing bring you joy? If it doesn't benefit you, and it doesn't help someone else, and it doesn't cause you joy, it's a nonstarter. But if it causes you joy, then throw caution to the wind and say yes. You'll figure the rest out.

Fourth, and most important, can (or better yet, should) someone else do it? We often say yes simply because we are asked—whether because we feel flattered, guilt-ridden, or trapped. But let's face it: quite often we are asked not because we were head-hunted and hand-selected as the best man or woman for the task, but simply because we made eye contact at the wrong time.

Subsume your ego, engage your intellect (and your Rolodex), and take a back seat if you aren't the right person for the job. Fret not—they'll find someone else. They always do. It turns out that, for some things, you're just not that important. And as an added bonus, saying no will reserve your time so you can do the things for which you really are that important.

Ask for Sightlines

Somewhere along your path from doer to leader will be a boss who mindlessly forwards an email or tosses out an idea with the intro *Wouldn't it be great if …?* And you'll find yourself scrambling to come up with ideas, present solutions, and innovate—all in a vacuum of information, the whole time wondering what on earth your boss could have meant, whether you are going in the right direction, or whether this new nightmare should even be prioritized. You will have no idea how this fool's errand connects to the strategic plan, the quarterly goals, or anything else.

When someone asks you to jump, is your knee-jerk reaction to pause only long enough to ask, "How high?" If so, remember that it's good practice not to race around for a solution before you even understand the question. Instead of grabbing what's merely an idea balloon and pulling it down to a place of honor at the very top of your to-do list, first stop and ask the sender for clarification about the purpose of the assignment. Learn exactly what success would look like, how you will know if you are achieving it, and when to call for help. Ask for more direct sightlines into how the work informs that calling you wish to serve. You will waste less time and effort, allowing you to get to work on projects that feel more connected.

Visualizing how your work is connected to success can also include asking to tag along to meetings, presentations, cocktail parties, and networking events—anything that might help you gain an understanding of the bigger picture and of how those in charge make decisions that affect your life. Executives often don't want to overly burden more junior staff, and will be delighted that you have shown interest. Not only are these events useful in building connection to the work, but the time you spend en route will help you build connection to the leader.

Go Smaller to Get Bigger

Working for an inspirational leader can fulfill connection, regardless of whether that leader is the prototypical loud, out-front, charismatic personality, or a quieter type who leads from behind. Either way, being close to the action can give you a sense of how such leaders work, how they think, and how they connect to your calling. And this might take the form of a role that is at a lower level but in a higher office.

Look for the box on the organizational chart that is as close to the action as you can find, even if it means taking a smaller job. Being an assistant in the CEO's office will show you more, teach you more, connect you more than being a division manager fourteen rungs down. If you want to be connected, you need to be in the room where it happens. You will get sightlines into not only how your work matters, but how every role in the organization matters, too.

Make Your Résumé Work for You

Humility, myopia, amnesia, and urgency are the four horsemen of the résumé apocalypse. Think back to any time (outside of that first post-graduation job search) when you've been asked for a résumé. As you sat down to update what you'd actually accomplished, you tried to strike a balance between pride and arrogance; to encapsulate all you can do under one job title; to remember everything you'd accomplished between *then* and *now*; and to finish updating it by the deadline. This wasn't an easy task, and that's why it's important to keep your résumé up to date even when you aren't in the market for a new job.

What's more, updating your résumé once a year or more will remind you of how your work matters—or will show you that it doesn't. But here's the trick: list your accomplishments, not your tasks. Don't write about all the action; write about the results that came from the action. Then consider those results carefully. If you can draw a direct line from your work to the calling that you are trying to serve, you have connection. If you can't, the holes you need to fill will become plain.

Don't discount the work you are doing outside of your specific job title. Remember to include work you may have done as a member of an ad hoc office committee, regardless of whether it involved your official duties. Examine your projects and highlight any and all skills you have developed while completing each of the tasks involved. Even if these skills and tasks don't seem relevant to your current job, they may be part of the bigger picture of consonance later.

And even if they aren't, or if you can't find connection, the assessment and inventory process of résumé upkeep will bolster your confidence in your skills, which can help you when you're ready to make that leap toward your calling.

Questions to Guide Your Search for Connection

Connected workers are the most engaged and the most successful. They are keen. They are energized. They take their work seriously because they understand the impact it has on their colleagues, the quarterly report, or the company mission.

Disconnected workers are just as easy to spot. They show up to work and complete their tasks, but they are the malcontent. They feel underappreciated, undervalued, and underpaid. Sometimes they're the ones who have lost steam along the way. And sometimes they're the ones who think they are kicking ass—and they truly are working hard, but they're building beautiful systems that end up operating in silos.

As you search for connection, consider the following questions:

- What would happen if you didn't show up to work today?
- Do you understand how the work you do connects with the problem you're trying to solve or the company you're trying to build?

- How much of your work is related to your goals?
- Do you know specifically what you need to do each day, and how doing it moves your goals forward?
- How does your success in your work translate to the success of the calling you are trying to serve?
- How does your relationship with the leader or manager factor into your connection?

Chapter 6

Contribution

I first met Jina Sanone when we worked together in the Clinton White House on the team that created AmeriCorps. Dabbling, like me, in politics, Jina always hoped her "real job" would be in the airline industry. After earning her MBA from the University of Michigan, she landed her dream job for Northwest Airlines, which later merged with Delta Airlines. Over the next seventeen years, Jina did work she loved and rose through the ranks, optimizing pricing strategies and leveraging alliance partnerships to increase revenue for a company, and in an industry, that she felt to be her calling. She worked with people whom she liked, on projects that she loved—including an internal initiative to build programs that developed women's leadership at all levels of the company—and in ways that brought out her very best, all while crisscrossing the globe thanks to the company's free travel perks. Jina loved her job.

But then a funny thing happened.

Jina found herself plateauing at work, called more to her interest in women's leadership and itching to get back into politics. She saw that women were not succeeding in the highest levels of politics as quickly as she had hoped, and it soon became clear to her that data—her bailiwick—was to blame.

Historically, women have been encouraged by a whole host of non-profits to run for office. The idea is that when more women run, more women win. But Jina disagreed. She saw evidence that this "boil the ocean" strategy wasn't working. Instead, it was leading to the cannibalization of already constrained resources, with women running for office regardless of whether the seat might be winnable.

So Jina took a leave of absence from Delta and started a nonprofit called Her Term, to analyze the data to determine in *which* districts women were likely to be most successful, and then recruit and train women from those specific districts to run and win.

This is where most stories of consonance might end with *happily ever after*. But Jina encountered an unexpected problem: she hated the fundraising process. Jina's nonprofit was not large enough yet to pay her, so she was missing the element of contribution in its most basic form: the level of income needed for the life she wanted to live. She faced an existential crisis.

Jina looked at her options and determined that she should return to a full-time position with Delta and support Her Term on the side. She was well-respected throughout the company, so the transition back would be relatively seamless. She returned to an industry that she still loved, but to a career that was less of a calling to her than before.

Now you might be thinking, *Well, this sounds terrible. It sounds like Jina is settling. This isn't how I want to achieve consonance.* But this story isn't intended to offer a fairytale Hollywood ending. Instead, it makes a specific point: Jina does have consonance, because after her calling shifted in 2016, she adjusted and achieved connection (via Her Term) as well as contribution (via Delta). She enjoys consonance in an overall picture of work that matters to her.

What Is Contribution?

The work we do should contribute something to our lives—but what? When we sit back and fantasize about the life we want to live, we all have different definitions of success. Some of us want to pay off our student loans. Some of us want to increase our vocational velocity. Some of us want our work to reflect and enhance the values we want to live by. Some of us want the access and power that privilege can afford. Some of us want to live a life in the service of others. And some of us want to realize some combination of all of these things and more.

And here's where contribution comes into play. Whereas connection is about how the work you do fulfills the calling you want to serve, contribution is all about you. Contribution is about how the work you do helps to build the life you want to live.

It is obvious that the woman whose job allows her to live her values at work and at home is in consonance. But who is to say that hers is the only way? Consider the man who works in a soul-sucking job because it pays for his beloved Lamborghini and weekend lake house. Who is to say that he has any less consonance than the guy who works a soul-sucking job because it allows him to donate money to curing cancer? Regardless of what you think of these individuals, their choices allow them to be limitless in how their work contributes to what they hold dear. And, frankly, they are the only ones who get a vote.

Reverence for a Whispered Dream

Every day, I hear from up-and-coming superstars with big-ass goals. They tell me about their methodology, their expectations, their ten-point plans of action. But I always listen for something else—that thing they keep buried deep inside, that whisper of the unspoken dream, that person they would want to be if what they did contributed to who they secretly imagined they could become.

You know which dream I mean: the one you dare not speak out loud. This is the dream that is so big, so scary, so bowel-shakingly audacious that you almost feel bad for wanting it. But you do want it. You really, really do. And having this dream—and having a reverence for this dream—well, that's the thing that tells me who is going to succeed and who is not. Because it is that reverence that tells me someone isn't just following his or her passion, but that they are willing to *invest* in that passion.

Owning the Dream

We all have goals that we think of as our own creation. But the truth is, most of them were set by someone else. Your parents told you to get good grades in school. Your boss tells you to want the big promotion. Your friends and neighbors pressure you to score the right spouse, drive the right car, live in the right apartment, wear the right clothes in exactly the right size. And on and on and on ...

All too often, we get caught up in the momentum of this external motivation by pleasing someone else, following the footsteps, doing what is expected. And we don't stop to wonder why.

What if you were being honest with yourself—truly, unflinchingly honest? What would you really want? What is the Big Hairy Audacious Goal you're willing to fight for? What will this path, this goal, this dream contribute to the life you want to lead?

In my experience, the most successful professionals are never the ones who simply want the next promotion to the next big job just because that's what is expected. Instead, they're the ones who are so hungry for their own self-determined goals that they are intrinsically motivated to go after them. The most flourishing, most fulfilled workers are the ones who do the extra work, in the dark, when no one sees—the ones who own up to their BHAGs and are willing to dig deep and fight like hell to bring them to fruition. They do it for themselves, because they want to achieve those goals so badly that they can't not do it. They know that leaning into those goals will contribute to the life they want to live, and they are insatiably hungry for that version of success. And you just can't be insatiably hungry for someone else's version of success, for someone else's goal, for someone else's cause.

In Praise of Ambition

Ambition has gotten a bad rap of late. It's a dirty word—even more so if you are a woman. (*Oh, she's so ambitious!*) Part of the reason we've lost ownership of our unspoken dreams is that we've been persuaded to allow our ambition to be subsumed into something that is more socially acceptable: faux humility.

Why do you want to get ahead? What do you want to do with that power? Do you want to change your family, your community, your country, your world? Do you want to make a mark, large or small, on this earth? What kind of life do you want to live? How do you want to raise your family? Do you want to give back? Will an elevated position, an increased salary, and a voice of leadership help you do this? Of course it will.

Yet the guilt of ambition holds us back and keeps us from becoming limitless. Somewhere along the way, we assigned sainthood to the word purpose, as if there were a picture of Mother Teresa next to its definition in the dictionary. And that's where the train began to career off the tracks.

If you look up the definition of purpose—and I did—it's pretty benign: Purpose is merely the reason for which something exists or why it is done. That's all. No picture of a saint, no finger-wagging friend, no "tsk-tsk" or assigning shame for not preceding it with the word higher. Nothing—and no one—is there saying that a job that helps you pay off your student loans faster, but fails to cure the world's ills, isn't purposeful.

Has it ever occurred to you that you owe it not only to yourself, but to everyone and everything you want to have an impact on to be ambitious in choosing and chasing your goals? If being in that elevated position, with that increased salary and that greater voice of leadership, allows you to make more of an impact on the very calling that you hold dear, it's more than just your ambition. It's your responsibility.

We find purpose in achieving our goals, whatever they may be. But here's the thing: Purpose has no judgement. Only we humans do. If crushing student loans are what's standing between you and the freedom of choice to live the life you want, if buying that convertible is what will bring you joy, if landing that promotion is part of your life's plan, then why not elevate your expectations of the contribution you require from your work?

Four Ways to Bring Contribution to Your Work

Stas Gayshan started his career in politics in pursuit of purpose through cause. He worked in terrible conditions for the quixotic campaigns of candidates who fed his passion and fueled his love for the bold, idealistic goal. But campaign work is hard, and at the end of it, the results are binary: You win or you lose. There is no second place. And when you lose, the pain is acute, real, and immediate. One day, you are firing everything in your arsenal; the next day, you are out of a job. And once you lose, it's hard not to look back and wonder if any of it was worth it.

Stas inhabited a working life where winning was happiness and losing was misery. He had to figure out another way to look at things, to determine whether any of the work mattered at all. He had to stop chasing happiness—and start chasing meaning.

Stas tried to focus on the positive that came from those campaigns, even the losing ones. He realized that progress had been made on various issues and in various districts. Sure, each campaign was embodied by a particular candidate, but he or she was merely the imperfect human vehicle for the portfolio of causes that Stas held dear. Sometimes the candidate lost, but nevertheless the issues lived on and were carried forth by the next candidate. Among his colleagues, too, there were meaningful moments: personal achievements, marriages and babies, and everlasting friendships.

Eventually Stas learned not to see failure as the finale, but rather as a point on his path to success. Point by point, he could continue to fight for the things that mattered to him alongside the people who inspired him. He adjusted his lens so that he could understand better the contribution each job brought to the life he wanted to live. As he did this, Stas realized that he could embody this calling more and feel a greater sense of this contribution if he figured out scalable solutions for both the candidates and the causes themselves.

Every campaign had the same handicap: When it came to building the back-office services, no one seemed to have the necessary expertise. Each new campaign staff was reinventing the wheel. So Stas started Space with a Soul, which offered shared offices, conference rooms, event spaces, and back-office services to campaigns and nonprofits alike.

Then Tim Rowe, founder and CEO of the innovation and coworking hub Cambridge Innovation Center (CIC), came knocking with a crazy, inspirational, audacious goal: scale CIC across the globe and provide space for nonprofits and for-profits alike to grow. Stas eagerly signed on. Now, Stas no longer serves candidates or nonprofits through full-time campaign work—though he still volunteers actively on the side. Instead, he answers his calling of making the world a better place, while enjoying a fuller essence of the contribution that he sought in politics.

Why do we misunderstand contribution? Why do we avoid going after what we want? And even when we do go after what we think we want, why do we still feel out of consonance? For too long, we've been told that good work must be work done for the greater good—and felt guilty for wanting something that didn't fit into that rubric.

Let's reset the expectations right here and right now. Your contribution is how your work creates the life you want to live, the lifestyle you want to have, and the values you want to uphold—not the goals laid out for you by others. But in order to feel as though the contribution piece of the equation is, in fact, contributing to the life you want, you have to start owning up to exactly what that life looks like.

Find Your Tribe

Are your goals for contribution similar to those of your coworkers? Can you discuss and share these goals, and recruit help toward achieving them, among the people with whom you spend the majority of your weekday waking hours? And, perhaps most importantly, are you able to be the authentic you during working hours, just as you are at home?

If your forty-hour-a-week vocation is merely what pays for your true avocation or advocacy, you will feel consonant only if this extracurricular activity isn't at odds with the goals of your coworkers or company. Cancer researchers probably won't find willing conversational partners to discuss their cigar club at work. Dental hygienists will be looked at askance when they ask colleagues to taste-test the results of their weekend candy-making hobby. Contribution leads to full consonance only when your goals are in alignment with the goals of those in your tribe.

Focus on Your Avocation

If you are finding that your avocation—that thing you love to do, even if it's not part of or related to your vocation—contributes more to the life you want to live than the job you have, it's time to shift your focus. You've heard the saying: *Figure out what you love, and then figure out how to get paid for it.* What is it about the avocation that works for you? Does it allow you to live in greater alignment with your values? Does your avocation govern the company you keep, the friends you make, the leaders that inspire you? Does it help you acquire skills or methods that improve your approach to other parts of your life?

Of course, sometimes it's hard to fully replace your vocation with your avocation, especially if that hobby is, say, bird watching or stamp collecting. (Cue the hate mail from the ornithologists and philatelists.) So if that type of move is out of reach for you, spend some time figuring out *why* you love what you love—perhaps your avocation offers creative freedom, joyful teamwork, or intellectual curiosity, for example. Then figure out how to build those components into your paying work.

Know Your Value

If you are honest with yourself and realize that, for you, contribution is derived through monetary rewards, the obvious step is to negotiate for more income. But how do you do that, outside of just asking? And how do you ask for a raise if you feel shy, guilty, or anxious about it?

First, determine the market comparables—the fair market value for someone with your experience, doing your job, in a similar industry and geographic location. This will give you some sense of a realistic asking price. Then you need to leave behind your price (and your baggage) and think about your value instead.

You have a salary, and you think that's your value, but it's really something else: your price. So, what's the difference between the two?

Early in my speaking career, I was offered what I considered to be a ridiculously large sum of money for a forty-minute keynote presentation. "I feel like the Wizard of Oz," I confessed to my husband, thinking of myself not as the big badass they see on stage, but the tiny lady behind the curtain. "It just feels so fake to get paid actual, real money for forty minutes of work."

He turned to me and said, with a face that can only be described as mystified, "No, you're getting paid for twenty-five years and forty minutes of work."

In other words, my price is my speaking fee, the cost of getting me on the stage before a conference full of people. My value, on the other hand, is the sum total of all the work I have done to get on that stage—and all the wisdom and presence and charisma that I bring to it.

If you are at a later point in your career, your value is the compounded wisdom of decades of experience—of successes and, yes, of failures, too. If you are just starting out, your value may be the time you are able to spend in a trial-and-error period of iteration, or the strong network of friends, mentors, and champions you gather around you—and learn from at breakneck speed.

At any point in your personal and professional evolution, it is never the momentary sprint of genius alone that makes you a valuable worker, but the many hard yards that came before it. What you are willing to accept is your price; what got you here is your value. Always negotiate your price based on your value.

Practice Gratitude

Years ago, I did work for Larry Fish, then CEO of the largest bank in New England. To prepare for our first meeting, I watched a talk he gave to an MBA class at the MIT Sloan School of Management, in which he mentioned that he started every Monday by writing a thank-you note to one of his staff. In our first meeting, I remarked on that, asking Larry how he found something to write about each and every week.

Larry looked me dead in the eye and said, "I have a thousand employees. If I can't find someone to whom I can express gratitude at least once a week, I'm not paying attention."

When you see others who are living your shared values through their work, take a moment to recognize and praise how they are doing this. The active practice of gratitude cements for you just what they are doing—and why it matters to you. Being openly grateful allows you to more intentionally increase how your daily actions at work contribute to the values you want to live by.

Likewise, you can do the same thing for your own actions. So often we look to work on what's broken, but by focusing also on what's going well, we can increase contribution by making our own actions intentional too. This will not only allow you to pay attention to the parts of your work that you want to grow; it will force you to focus on what you actually think is additive.

Questions to Guide Your Search for Contribution

Some will interpret contribution as a flexible schedule that allows new parents to spend quality time with their children. Some will interpret it as working in a job that affords them the highest possible salary so that they can be active philanthropists or rabid, carefree consumers (or both!). And some hope that their work contributes to putting them in the company of people who inspire them to be a better friend, parent, or spouse.

Here's the kicker: they are all right.

Contribution merely means that you understand how the work that you do allows, enables, and empowers you to become limitless by positioning you to be more of the person you want to be. As you search for the way that you want your work to contribute to your life, consider the following questions:

- Does your job afford you the lifestyle that you want?
- How do you want your work to contribute to the life you want to live?
- Does your work give deeper meaning to your spiritual needs or community values?
- Do the values of your work life align with the values of your home life?

- Would you be satisfied making less money if the work you did felt more aligned with your values?
- In what ways do you need greater freedom or flexibility in your work environment?
- What intangible rewards would you want in exchange for, or in addition to, the current monetary rewards of your career?

Chapter 7

Control

Leslie Ehm was a musician and a television host and a script editor, spending the days of her early career in highly collaborative and creative teams. It lit her up; it fueled her soul. Then she moved into advertising, lured by the talk of even more collaborative creativity—and quickly became frustrated. Her colleagues talked a big game, but she saw no evidence of it in action. She decided that, rather than working in a creative company, she wanted to teach people how to be collaboratively creative.

Leslie had to figure out how to execute her calling in a way that was consonant with who she was, a headstrong and untrainable person with precious little background in the psychology of training. So, rather than trying to do it the way that others had done it, she decided to build a training course that would have worked for her, breaking it down into the smallest of steps, unpacking the process so that it would be tangible. And it worked. She was successful beyond her wildest dreams, until she found herself on the horns of a dilemma: continue to do what she was doing, what she had been doing happily and successfully for the previous five years, or grow bigger, responding to the overwhelming demand she was getting from the market.

Not growing wasn't a viable option for Leslie, a woman who was constantly on the lookout for bigger, better, faster, more. Being content with the status quo would not have been consonant to her. But she couldn't imagine anyone else doing what she did, the way that she did, as well as she did. She feared that if she couldn't replicate what she did, then the magic wasn't the intellectual property she created, it was her. She didn't want to be "The Leslie Show," so she took Door #2, slowly hiring staff and even more slowly training them.

What happened next surprised Leslie. She thought that what she liked to do was the training, to see the clients light up when they had the a-ha moment about what she was teaching. But she also knew that she needed new challenges in order to stay connected to her work. It led her to her fuller calling: not just teaching collaborative creativity, but hiring people and giving them a shot at finding their own greatness. She learned that in order to feel limitless, she needed to be able to control who she hired, how she trained them, and how they became exceptional vessels to deliver knowledge to their clients. When she had this control, she was able to fulfill her truest calling of bringing out the greatness in others.

Why Do We Need Control?

"I'd like to ride that terrifying roller coaster of unknown length, in the dark, for an uncertain number of times, without any guarantee that my seatbelt is fully functioning or that the ride has been inspected anytime in the past ten years," said no one ever.

I'm not ashamed to say that I don't like roller coasters at all, not even when I'm sure that the seatbelt works and the inspection certificate is up to date. I am a control freak of the highest magnitude. But even those who do enjoy thrill-seeking in their personal life probably need to feel that they have some element of control over their work.

Autonomy matters. In fact, it matters so much that the degree to which you have control—over the work you do, the team with which you do it, and the projects on which you are engaged—has a direct impact on your performance at work. And these days, workers tend to expect more autonomy and control over their work. Technology in particular has opened up new opportunities for us to do all kinds of work and to do it from anywhere—our offices, our cars, or the other side of the globe.

Having confidence in our level of self-determination at work allows us to control our world, to feel protected and safe, and to know that we have options. Control is so important that various studies have shown workers would be more likely to take a job that gives them more control instead of a job that gives them more power.[13]

So, why do we still feel as though we are limited by our lack of control? Why do we have trouble connecting *what we do* with *who we are*? What keeps us from influencing the contribution that work makes to our lives? It starts when we accept an early and perhaps incomplete definition of *who we should be*.

Short-Shrifting Self-Discovery

Even though you are being proactive by reading this book as part of your process of becoming limitless, you should know that you, like all of us, have actually been getting in your own way for a long time. You have limited yourself.

Certainly, this isn't intentional. It's not that we don't know which way to go next. It's that we are attempting to build a path forward based on the coordinates that mark where we've already been. And so far, our aim has been way off.

We are giving short shrift to the self-discovery process. It should come as no surprise that most of us have trouble navigating toward consonance. Our voyage to self-discovery was commandeered long ago.

---

13 According to research published in 2013 on autonomy and its relation to work outcomes, as cited in Belle Beth Cooper, "The Key to Happiness at Work Isn't Money—It's Autonomy," *Quartz*, May 4, 2016, https://tinyurl.com/ya5zf9u4.

Your Teachers Were Probably Wrong

Back in middle school, you were taught to pursue the gold stars, get the good grades, and shine across the board. You had no say in the skills that got rewarded; often what you were rewarded for was different from what you loved. And, of course, you had to be good at every subject. Right brain or left brain, be damned! You were only as smart and as valuable as the average of your grade points across every subject. It didn't matter if you loved numbers or if you were turned on by words; specialization was irrelevant in fourth grade.

Then, suddenly, at seventeen or eighteen years old, you were told to pick a college, pick a major, pick a trade, pick a life path. And you know what's crazy about that? At age eighteen, your frontal lobe—the very part of your brain that determines good decision-making—wasn't even fully formed yet.

So, rather than picking a path based on what makes us special—what we like, what we do well, and where we shine—most of us are forced to pick our path early, based on values attached by others and on interests that aren't our calling. Our teachers tossed out career path options based on not much more than anecdotal information gathered at a specific moment in time. They possessed no crystal ball, and yet we internalized their notions as predictions rather than simply suggestions.

If you're still operating on career assumptions arbitrarily handed out decades ago, it's probably time to get your hands on the wheel, take control of the ship, and start charting your own course.

"Fake It 'Til Ya Make It" Sucks

Fake it 'til ya make it posits that if we pretend to be something, we will eventually become it. Well, I think that's a bunch of hooey. Ever notice that this so-called wisdom tends to be proffered by those whose best advice is *Just hustle harder*? "Faking it" is not the right path to self-discovery, for two reasons.

First, how do you even know what you want to fake when you don't have any idea of what would be consonant to who you are, to how you define calling? Without a clear direction—a steadfast little lighthouse beckoning and guiding you—modeling your actions to suit that purpose will be next to impossible. This is especially true if you are still taking your cues from whatever professional path your algebra teacher once thought might be suitable for you.

Second, while you are so busy faking it, you won't get a chance to let down your guard and allow yourself to practice—and to fail. Without the opportunity afforded by failure, you have no chance to reset, recalibrate, and restart. If you're pretending you're already on the right path, how will you expand your skills or explore your options?

I was twenty-two years old when I walked into the White House. I remember looking around and seeing the other bright young things buzzing around the office, full of purpose, with dog-eared newspapers in their briefcases, furiously writing their brilliant ideas on notepads just in time for meetings. So I did the same. I would read the papers from front to back, attempting to absorb it all. I'd sit at the table writing down notes about things that were mostly irrelevant. And all the while, I was missing the conversations happening around me, the relationships I should have been forming, the information I could have onboarded. I was trying so hard to look smart that I wasn't actually being smart.

Years later, at my own firm, I would find myself sitting at client pitches watching my staff members trying to act like me, talk like me, move like me. It didn't work for them. They weren't me, and so they would never be good at being me. This didn't make them failures, of course; it just made them failures at the art of imitation. Once they stopped acting like me and started acting like themselves, they learned to find their own voices. That's when they started to soar.

When we build models of leadership for ourselves that sit on the foundation of "fake it 'til ya make it," we put limits on our growth.

Emulating others only stifles your own brand of courage. You can't learn how to be confident when your success feels not like yours, but instead like an imitation of others.

There is no shortcut to discovering and mastering your own voice, to exploring your own consonance, and to finding the life that you consider to be of consequence.

Defining Quality

As the CEO of my own executive search firm, from time to time staff members would wonder why I was unhappy with their work even when the client seemed satisfied. "The client liked it, so what's the problem?" they'd ask.

The problem was that our clients had not seen good work from the firms they'd hired in the past. That was why we were getting the at-bat, after all. Should we have rested on our laurels just because our work was 5 percent better? Well, that didn't fit into my calling, and it certainly fell short of my idea of contribution. I wanted to build a better firm than that, and I wanted to live my values of doing extremely high-quality work. Our clients didn't get to decide that the work was "good enough," because they had no historical reference point to measure what was good enough.

In our firm, the measurements of excellence were clearly articulated. It was my firm, and I got to set the rules. As the CEO, I was in control. But in your life, you are the CEO of something: you. Do you know what your measurements of success are? And is your work allowing you to have control over them?

Four Ways to Bring Control to Your Work

Tara Diab started working on construction sites when she was twelve years old, picking up nails, cleaning up trash, and fetching whatever anyone wanted. Sometimes, the guys working the site would show her what they were doing. She loved everything about it. It was her calling.

As a young carpenter, Tara worked for her brother-in-law as he started to grow his commercial flooring business. One of the things he taught her was that if, at the end of the day, you can look back and say, "That's good enough"—well, you had better take the time to go back and do it again, with a little more pride. That work ethic stuck with Tara.

The only problem was that as her brother-in-law's business started to grow, that ethic wasn't always shared by his workers. The company never wavered in its commitment to excellence, but managing employees who had a "paycheck over perfection" attitude was not how Tara wanted to spend her time. It wasn't that the employees were doing it wrong; it was that they didn't take the extra time to get it just right.

Tara felt that she didn't have enough control over the quality of work output, and a business model that forced her to compromise between time and talent made her feel less connection to her work. She wasn't sure how to move forward. The work wasn't contributing to the kind of person she wanted to be and the kind of life she wanted to live.

And then the decision was made for her when the economy tanked and the business suffered, forcing Tara to figure out what to do next. She took on odd jobs here and there—anything that would pay her, really, whether it was hanging pictures or refinishing cabinets. She lived like this for five years, month by month, never sure of whether or not she'd be able to make ends meet. Meanwhile, she worked on her own custom furniture design. Eventually, those odd jobs became regular jobs, and the regular jobs became bigger jobs, until at last she was able to feel confident that Diab Custom Design was for real.

Now Tara calls the shots, with the integrity she felt was missing from contractors whose business got so big that they lost control of the quality. She infuses that integrity into everything she does, from the relationships with clients to the apprentices she hires and trains— just ask my teenage son, who worked summer construction for her.

Tara has her calling firmly in mind; is connected to the way the work builds her business; sees how the income and the integrity contribute to the life she wants to live; and is able to control exactly how the work gets done. Her dance card is always booked twelve months in advance and she works all the time, but she says it never feels like work.

So, how can *you* get more control—the agency to influence the level of connection and contribution that your work gives you in pursuit of your calling?

See Failure as Fulcrum, Not Finale

The fear of failure limits our ability to get ourselves right, to determine who we are when we are at our very best—to groove the pattern as a leader when we are that best self. If we try to prevent failure by acting like we know what we're doing, we will groove that pattern instead of *acting* like we know what we are doing. We won't actually learn how to do it. Nor will we learn why and how it works—or whether or not we actually find that work personally meaningful.

Being good at something and finding that thing purposeful are not one and the same. Equating the two perpetuates the same empty pursuit of gold stars for something that doesn't sing to you. Instead, give yourself permission to fail. Try to stop seeing failure as a finale, as definitional. Instead, start seeing failure as a fulcrum—a turning point from which to become limitless.

You may think that if you keep faking it, you can never fail. But this setup forces you to speak using other people's voices, and to act using other people's mannerisms. You try to control for everything and end up controlling nothing. Rather than holding more tightly to the reins, you need to allow space for trying out new things, for failure and feedback. This approach will offer greater insight into the areas where you are in consonance, so you can focus on what really matters and gain traction over those things.

Take Serena Williams as an example. Serena is one of the fiercest competitors ever to grace the tennis court (or any athletic stage, for that matter), and yet in practice, she doesn't spend all her time working on what she has perfected. She does some of that, of course, to groove the pattern. But spending more time being uncomfortable—fixing what's not working, going deep into the pain cave and facing her failures—ensures that she can always come out stronger.

Each of us can do the same thing, and find our own consonance in the journey.

Find Your Fundamental State of Leadership

Think of a time when you were at your very best—not just doing well, but really at your best, firing on all cylinders, inspiring action, closing the deal, making it rain. Or it could be a time when you were simply there in a quiet moment for a friend, sweeping your future spouse off his or her feet, or sitting with an aging and fearful parent during an unexpected medical procedure. This is what Professor Robert E. Quinn describes, in an influential 2005 Harvard Business School article, as your "fundamental state of leadership."[14]

That moment of perfect flow doesn't have to be in the workplace. But it needs to be a time when you were invincible, a moment when everything you do well was being called upon, when you were fully present and serving the need at hand. You were limitless.

As you think about such a moment in your life, recall the qualities you exhibited, the level of noise you made, the audience you addressed, the skills you used. Make a list of this evidence of your leadership and tape it to your computer, or make it the lock screen on your phone, or put it on the dashboard in your car. Read this list again and again. The constant reminder will turn these haphazard manifestations of your brilliance into muscle memory, and you will find yourself living the best and highest version of yourself.

---

14 Robert E. Quinn, "Moments of Greatness: Entering the Fundamental State of Leadership," *Harvard Business Review*, July–August 2005.

Set Up a Feedback Loop

Many of us feel a lack of control because of two competing forces: managers often dread giving us feedback, and in the absence of informed stories we create monsters. We adhere to mistaken priorities at work. We don't know where to improve. We spin our wheels. We could be better—we could do work that feels purposeful—if only someone would point us in the right direction.

So, why do managers hate feedback so much, and what can we do to fix that for them (and for us)?

Feedback is often a one-way communiqué, and is often awkwardly and randomly scheduled at times when the projects and processes being reviewed are distant memories. The most recent mistakes drown out the earlier successes. Your review session feels out of your control, and that doesn't feel good.

You need to take back control of the review process by creating a feedback loop. Sit down with your manager. Make a list of shared goals. Determine your supervisor's priorities for your work and ask for the resources you will need to meet them within the timeline expected. Then, loop back frequently to discuss progress. You will get more frequent, more relevant, and more timely feedback, which will let you control how your work impacts your career and salary growth.

Schedule a Framily Meeting

Gather your "framily" and unpack your goals. Never heard of your framily? It's the combination of your actual family and the friends who act like family, those ride-or-die types who tell you what you need to hear in the ways that you need to hear it. The beloved members of your framily, whoever they may be, are the best mirror to reflect whether the work you are doing matters.

Tell them your passions. Tell them your worries. Tell them about your income goals and your career growth goals. Tell them what is holding you back. Tell them about the values you want to live into through the work that you do. And then ask them to help ensure that the work you are doing comports with your goals as you have laid them out.

This isn't your typical "personal board of advisors" advice. Those folks—the mentors and the champions and even the naysayers—are there to help you navigate the career you wish to build. What you share with your framily is more personal, more vulnerable than that. But beware and be ready. When you talk to a fifteen-year-old about what is important to you and what is stopping you, it's going to get real—and real, real quick.

Questions to Guide Your Search for Control

Control can come in many forms, from input on performance metrics to salary and perks to workspace design. For some, control is the flexibility to manage the burdens of the sandwich generation— those of us who are taking care of both young kids and aging parents. For others, it's having a say in the kinds of leaders under whom you work. Perhaps you are seeking direct control over how hard you work and how much money you earn through sales and commissions. Or you may require greater influence over whether your working pace looks more like the roller coaster or the merry-go-round.

When we have our calling firmly in place ... and when we can connect the work we do to serving that calling ... and when we understand how that work contributes to the life we want to live ... finally, we need to have some ability to control how we go about our work.

As you seek control, consider the following questions:

- Do you want more say in larger companywide decisions?
- Do you feel as though your opinion matters?
- Do you know what you do well, and do you have a sense of how you could do more of it?

- Are you able to get your hands on the necessary resources to get your work done?
- What type of input do you have in the projects that you are handed or the teams with which you work?
- Are you empowered to seek feedback and mentoring from a variety of sources?
- Do you have any ability to influence the amount of money earned or the number of hours worked?
- Who is in your "framily," and how can you involve them more in what matters to you?

PART THREE

FINDING YOUR CONSONANCE

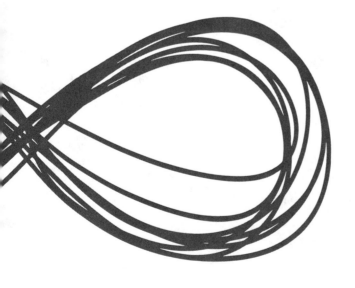

Chapter 8

Changing Your Career

I consider Dolly Parton to be my very own personal life coach, even though she and I have never actually met. (Girlfriend, if you're reading this: call me!)

Dolly once famously said, "Find out who you are, and do it on purpose." And really, can you think of anyone else on earth who did so well at finding out who she was and doing it on purpose—and damned unapologetically, at that—than Dolly Parton? She is practically limitlessness incarnate.

But, unlike Dolly, most of us spend our time shoehorning ourselves into other people's definitions of success, in pursuit of the gold stars we hope they'll deem us worthy of receiving. Then we measure our worth based upon our haul—how high we jumped, how fast we ran, how precisely we toed the line. We evaluate our performance based on how well we executed their version of success instead of on what is truly important to us.

We have allowed ourselves to fall into the trap of determining our value based on what other people consider valuable. What a load of crap that is! And we have no one but ourselves to blame.

So, what can we do about it?

For starters, you can have an honest conversation with yourself about who you are when you are at your best. Being someone else's idea of success only makes you a lesser version of yourself. Striving to fulfill your own definition, on the other hand, will compel you to be more than you ever expected.

Given the choice between lesser and more, I pick more every time.

Dolly sure knows how to be more: more sequins, more makeup, more silicone, more acrylic, more latex, more of whatever is in those wigs. This is who she is, and she is living it with every fiber (natural or not) of her being. And look how many gold stars (and gold records) she's (ahem!) racked up.

This is where we discover our power to become limitless. When we show up to work wearing other people's clothes, pretending to be something we are not, faking it 'til we make it—we are constraining ourselves. We are at odds with ourselves.

Dolly, as wonderful as she is, doesn't make sense singing the aria from Carmen at the Metropolitan Opera of New York. She knows which spotlights shine best upon her blonde tresses, and this provides her with a consonance that can't be beaten (even by Jolene). She can be entirely, wonderfully, audaciously Dolly.

For you to find consonance, you must understand which spotlights shine best upon you, too—when your energy is aligned with your tasks, when your goals are aligned with your desired outcomes, and when you can be, like Dolly, entirely, wonderfully, audaciously yourself. And you can't do that without some of each of the four fixed elements of calling, connection, contribution, and control.

Until now, this book has focused on these elements, and how much of each of the four you need in your life so that you can be in consonance and become limitless. Now let's consider whether your solution requires changing your career (this chapter), changing your workplace (chapter 9), or changing yourself (chapter 10).

Finding Consonance in Nonprofits

Changing your career can provide the satisfaction of a radical shift, one that reminds us that we have agency over what we perceive to be our limits. And the most radical, purpose-seeking career shift of all is turning your career upside down and going in a completely different direction: transitioning from corporate to nonprofit work.

A crisis of consonance—*I hate my job! Something is missing! Is this all there is?*—is often fueled by a lack of calling. And when it is, we drive straight to the land of purpose. Surrounding ourselves with others who demand more calling can bolster our connection and contribution as well.

Here's the good news: growth in the nonprofit sector has outpaced growth in the private and government sectors over the past thirty years.[15] And, as anyone in the corporate sector knows, growth means opportunity. But where does this growth come from, and what does it mean for your career change?

---

15 According to the nonprofit membership association Independent Sector, between 1987 and 2005, despite lagging behind in investment in infrastructure and talent development, nonprofits in the United States grew in number at nearly triple the rate of the business sector. Even more impressive is that nonprofit-sector employment grew 2.6 percent during 2007–2008, the first year of the recession, while corporate-sector employment shrank 1.1 percent. Nonprofit employment grew again by 1.2 percent in 2008–2009, while corporate employment shrank 6.2 percent. Philanthropy News Digest, "Growth in Nonprofit Employment Outpaces Rate in Private Sector," May 27, 2004, https://tinyurl.com/yaszhp4l.

A New Landscape for Talent and Funding

In 2006, the nonprofit consulting group Bridgespan published a sector-shaking study predicting a mass exodus of executives, those baby boomers responsible for creating and leading many of the nation's nonprofits. The sector had to come to terms with a new talent landscape by investing in leadership capacity, refining management rewards to attract and retain top talent, and expanding recruiting horizons while fostering individual career mobility. Nonprofits collectively began to dig in and do the work—and then the subprime housing crisis hit, and many of these soon-to-be retirees opted for another tour of duty.

As the market regained strength, the expected rate of nonprofit executive transition also bounced back, producing waves of leadership turnover unparalleled in the history of the sector and leaving nonprofits scrambling for experienced managers. More than just causing change at the top, this leadership vacuum created ripple effects, sending similar waves of turnover throughout every level of the organizational chart—and heralding unprecedented opportunity for those who are looking to transition from corporate to nonprofit work.

Adding to this encouraging trend is a major change in nonprofit fundraising in the form of two new breeds of funders. The first group are activist philanthropic tech billionaires who can make seismic transformational gifts. The second type of donors are millennials, who give individually but only after thorough internet research on where their donations can make the greatest impact. Both of these funders are pushing nonprofits to think more about metrics than ever before.

As a result of these demographic shifts, nonprofits have begun to look increasingly toward the corporate sector to recruit metrics-oriented managers and data-driven storytellers to satisfy their talent needs and, ultimately, their donors. Perhaps this includes you?

Welcoming Corporate Candidates

As the staffing needs of nonprofits have multiplied, and as the mind-sets of the funders have shifted, hiring corporate employees into the sector—at all levels—has become a common practice. Throughout my recruiting career, I saw an increasing number of requests, year after year, specifically for candidates transitioning from the corporate world.

Nonprofits today are both more flexible about the types of candidates they recruit and more broad-thinking about the skills those candidates bring on board. Candidates with experience in rapid-growth environments, expertise in management that is nurturing while still results-driven, and a history of actively grooming internal staff thrive in the nonprofit sector. This sounds familiar, doesn't it? It aptly describes, in large part, job-seekers from the corporate sector who not only have the requisite skills, but who seek to match what they do with who they are.

Dave Swensen pioneered this type of transition decades ago, well before it was the norm in the nonprofit sector. The son and grandson of college professors, Dave was at Yale University getting his PhD in economics and assuming he would teach once he'd finished his thesis on the corporate bond market. But then Salomon Brothers, where he had been gathering much of the data for his thesis work, offered him a job.

It was an exciting time on Wall Street, with a fresh group of quantitatively minded professionals revitalizing the once-sleepy bond market, and Salomon Brothers was the epicenter of this new wave. Fascinated by the intellectual appeal of being part of this groundbreaking time in financial markets, Dave said yes to the job. Still, he missed Yale and went back to teach a class every year.

Noticing this pull to the university, the provost asked Dave to take over management of the school's endowment. The offer came with an 80 percent pay cut, but Dave saw an opportunity to serve an institution that he loved while undertaking an intellectually reward-ing challenge: to fundamentally reshape the traditional approach to institutional investment management.

In this new role, Dave was able to apply the skills and knowledge from Wall Street to tackle similarly interesting problems in an aca-demic environment, generating resources for his beloved alma mater while completely revolutionizing the way institutions manage their portfolios.

Coming from the corporate sector, Dave not only carved out a space where he could put his ideas into practice while following his strong moral compass, but he developed a philosophy and manage-ment style that is now considered the gold standard in his industry. Yale's endowment has grown from $1 billion to more than $29 billion today, greatly increasing funding support for the mission of the uni-versity. Endowment spending now covers more than one-third of the operating budget, up from 10 percent when Dave came on board.[16]

It all started with Dave's calling to Yale, his connection to the work he was doing, the contribution to how this work allowed him to live his values, and his ability to control how the work was done.

* * * * *

As we've discussed throughout this book, transitioning from corpo-rate to nonprofit work is an excellent path for some. But it is not the only path. For others whose personality, mindset, or economics don't align, nonprofits might even be the wrong path. What mat-ters is that your choice aligns with your motivations and goals. This sense of shared purpose with people whose career paths run parallel to yours creates a solidarity that leads to more productivity and long-term satisfaction. You might find this in nonprofit work, or it could mean a shift to—or within—the corporate world.

---

16 Marc Gunther, "David Swensen's Guide to Sleeping Soundly," *Yale Alumni Magazine*, March/April 2009, http://archives.yalealumnimagazine.com/issues/2009_03/swensen.html.

Finding Consonance in the Corporate World

What if your career transition is motivated by an overwhelming urge for more calling, but you don't have a temperament or skill set that works well in the nonprofit sector? Rest assured, there are still plenty of ways to create social impact, even without compromising your personal economic value or your operating environment comfort level. This means either shifting the role you play in your current company, or finding a company that (like my search firm) is cause-driven but profit-focused.

Do Good While Doing Well

Laura Acosta was at a leadership retreat run by her law firm when she realized she needed a change. She and her colleagues were being put through an exercise about affinities. Her results kept reminding her that what she liked, and did best, was working with people in their efforts toward professional development. The problem was, at the time, she was knee-deep in a securities litigation career, working with typical class action cases: nameless, faceless plaintiffs on one side and a massive company on the other. Laura felt no connection between the work she was doing and the outcome of the case for the plaintiffs. There was no human element.

Then her dad, who had always been the picture of health, got sick. Within just six months he was dead. Laura felt acutely the need to love what she did, and in her current work she simply didn't. It had her on call all the time, taking her away from her family too often. She knew that she couldn't continue in securities litigation, yet she wasn't qualified to join the firm's professional development team. Even so, she loved the firm, was the family breadwinner, and didn't want to leave.

Rather than changing companies, Laura created a better place for herself in her firm. She made steps internally, first to the firm's employment law practice, where she explored her passion for diversity and advised clients on corporate diversity issues. Then her dream job opened up: managing diversity within her own firm. Now she builds and implements professional development for members of the firm, inculcating diversity and inclusion into the firm's employment practices.

In this job, Laura is able to fulfill her calling to work in diversity, inclusion, and professional development. She has control over her time, working in-house hours instead of pulling all-nighters. And she enjoys the contribution of living her values without having to sacrifice the income or benefits awarded by big firm work. She sees a direct connection between the work she does and the firm's bottom line, and she is no longer limited by the false choice between doing good and doing well.

Pursue Companies with Heart

In 2015, Shawn Askinosie turned his back on a successful career as a criminal defense attorney to start a chocolate factory that sourced 100 percent of its beans from local farmers around the world. His company's mission: to serve the farmers who grow the cacao beans, to make great chocolate, and to leave the world a better place than they found it.

Askinosie Chocolate sustainably feeds 1,600 students per day in Tanzania and the Philippines based solely on the income thrown off from buying from local farmers. Shawn isn't just a real-life Willy Wonka; he's the Willy Wonka of corporate social responsibility.

If you feel strongly that your work should reflect your life's values, but you want to stay within the corporate world, seeking a position within a socially responsible business is a promising alternative. Companies with heart give substantial consideration not just to their economic value but to their social mission as well.

Corporate social responsibility—using ecologically sustainable materials and insisting on fair labor practices, for example—may mean shaving off some profits in exchange for doing what is right.

Companies that practice what they preach have what is sometimes considered a "double bottom line": responsibility to both shareholder and cause.

Often, the social mission raises the profile of the business, thus raising the economic value in turn. Companies with socially responsible charters also find that they are better able to retain staff and to align management and board requirements with shareholder demands. As an important added bonus, they may create brand loyalty for reasons above and beyond product quality.

Whether a company was founded on social value principles or has only recently internalized corporate social responsibility as part of its mission and vision, it may be the right place for you if it's able to turn its pursuit of purpose into an employment proposition for potential staff.

Here are just a few examples in several industries:[17]
- Consumer goods: Eileen Fisher, Procter & Gamble, The Body Shop
- Food: Ben & Jerry's, Newman's Own, Stonyfield Farms
- Finance: The Calvert Group, NorthStar Asset Management, Putnam Investments
- Service: Bright Horizons, United Parcel Service, Working Assets

Then there are the companies that get all up in their employees' business, using the economic levers at their disposal to socially engineer the world they'd like to see. For some companies, this approach might mean crafting human resources policies that are as universally acceptable as paying employees to quit smoking or lose weight, thus

17 More examples can be found at Business for Social Responsibility (www.bsr.org) and at Social Venture Network (www.svn.org).

promoting a healthier culture overall. Other companies take it even further, getting more hands-on with their activism through the allocation of their profits to causes they champion.

Companies like this exist on both ends of the political spectrum. Hobby Lobby cited the Christian values of its founders when removing the coverage of abortions from its employee healthcare policy, and took the fight to retain this right all the way to the Supreme Court. WeWork, one of the fastest-growing coworking spaces, announced in 2018 that it would no longer reimburse employee meals with meat in them. No matter where you stand, you can find a company that will allow your work to contribute to your consonance by speaking volumes about who you are.

Consider Corporate Philanthropy

Corporate philanthropy provides another opportunity for companies to exhibit their values, as McDonald's does with the Ronald McDonald House Charities. Jobs in this area can be found in company foundations, in the external affairs offices of chief executives, or elsewhere—even where you least expect them.

Toni Schwarzenbach Burke had no interest in changing careers. She was the executive director of City Year San José, a nonprofit that places volunteers in low-performing schools to create environments of excellence and improve student outcomes. Toni was sitting pretty, having just completed a capital fundraising campaign. And then Bill McDermott, chief executive officer of the multinational software corporation SAP, asked her to join his team as the head of external affairs for the office of the CEO.

Toni had never expected to work in the corporate world, but this offer seemed too good to refuse. She would get to divide her time between ensuring that the CEO was leveraged to influence thought leadership, policy change, and community support. And with the new position came a lucrative corporate salary.

Determining whether or not the position made sense for her demanded that Toni question her certainty about what gave her purpose. Could she be of service in a role that wasn't in a nonprofit organization? Would she find consonance in the corporate world?

In the end, Toni said yes. Today, she is no longer limited by her salary as a nonprofit executive. Her work not only allows her to continue in a life of service, but contributes to her ability to care for her young family and her aging father. Toni is also pleased that she can now personally offer financial support to the causes she loves.

Toni's position also gives her the opportunity to direct resources, both intellectual and financial, from SAP to those important causes. She lives the values she holds dear by placing the CEO, a leader who inspires her, in rooms where he can support policy changes that are consonant with who Toni is and strives to be. Even though she doesn't get to see kids bopping into their City Year schools every morning, Toni can be connected in different ways as she volunteers her time mentoring the organization's new executive director and leadership team, all while making a difference globally with SAP.

Aligning yourself with a company that manifests your values through its philanthropy is a direct path to fulfilling your calling, connection, and contribution, while giving you control, too.

Determining What's in Your Toolkit

If you determine that you need to change your career, fret not. All is not lost. You have skills, education, and training that will transfer to your new career or your new sector. Let's explore each of them and consider how you may be able to use them to become limitless.

Transferable Skills

Which of your skills are transferable? That depends somewhat on your field and your position in that field, but the simple answer is: all of them. Every skill you use in your current working situation can be used in work that matters more to you.

It's possible, even probable, that you will need to pick up some new skills to participate fully in the new role you'd like to play. But for the most part you'll find that you already have most of what it takes to get started. Whether your toolkit includes hard skills like management or knowledge of the law, or softer skills such as empathy and organization, isn't all that significant. Transferring your skills is less about changing content and more about changing your context.

Although you may need to learn some new rules or technological points—depending on your company's tax bracket—most duties that fall under the operations, administration, and finance functions are easily transferable. To do fundraising and advocacy work, you might have to adjust to some legal differences around the tax code. But for the most part, these practical skills will be easily transportable into the new work that you seek.

Other skills, like community building and fund development, transfer well after a bit of tweaking. Charisma, confidence, and persuasiveness know no tax bracket or organizational chart limit. And selling stocks may not be the same as raising money for a nonprofit—pushing karmic reward takes a tactic that differs from promising profit margins—but in each case you are following the same footwork: Do the research, be the steward, ask, and follow up.

Skills that are heavily reliant on subject matter expertise are much more difficult to transfer, but this is still not an impossible route. For example, a marketing director focused on selling to educational outfits may be able to bring a quiver full of both functional and subject-matter arrows to a job raising money for a charter school association

On the other hand, an ophthalmologist will bring a deep understanding of the medical community and its efforts to support blind children, but a lifetime of clinical expertise will not be useful when attempting to budget, deal with funders, or sign off on press releases. Those skills must (and can) come from elsewhere. In such cases, consider a halfway measure. For example, the eye doctor could open up a portion of his existing practice to serving low-income patients.

Formal Education

If you don't have a great deal of work experience, your formal education determines what, substantively speaking, you are qualified to do. This entails the whole of your subject matter expertise. For those who are just coming out of school or who have a short job history under their belts, education is of paramount importance and will be weighted heavily by the hiring manager. What you know matters, and at this point what you know has come mainly from your schooling.

For those who have been in the working world a bit longer, education is only one part of the equation. In some cases, like medicine or the law, a formal degree is a state requirement. Social workers and teachers must be licensed, and stock traders and accountants must pass certain exams. (We are not savages, after all.) In other cases, like fundraising or association management, a degree or certificate is not a requirement, but it provides a leg-up against other candidates.

In some roles, a deep, substantive knowledge of the work being done is vital to a candidate's success once on board. This is often borne out by a long career in the field, especially in cases where attaining more education is unrealistic. You are unlikely to enter medical school when you are forty-five years old, although certainly it has been done. And if you work in law or finance, you're probably not going to up and decide to get a PhD in oceanography to work at the Jacques Cousteau Foundation (however much fun that may sound).

In other cases, degrees that teach skills and not subject matter expertise—such as programs on nonprofit management, fundraising, accounting, and operations, or certificates in entrepreneurship, teaching, or health coaching (like fitness and nutrition)—are easily attainable and make sense strategically. It's simply a matter of determining whether the investment of time and money will give you the return you seek, whether karmic or financial.

On-the-Job Training

Many job-seekers have received enough on-the-job training to write a doctoral thesis on the work they do. Even if this is true in your working life, you probably don't realize how much you've learned along the way. Figuring out just how much expertise you've acquired and absorbed demands critical thinking about where you came from, your initial expectations of your career trajectory, and where you have ended up.

- What did you hope to get from your career? Are you there?
- What changed along the way?
- What do you do now that you never imagined you would be doing?
- What do you know more about now than when you started this job ... or the last job ... or the job before that?

As you take a deep dive into your memory (and résumé) while considering questions like these, don't forget about the community service, nonprofit volunteering, or board work that you've performed. Each of your days has brought a lesson, and each lesson is valuable to your job search in some way.

What lessons have you learned along the way?

Chapter 9

Changing Your Workplace

When I launched my firm, I did so with a six-week-old infant in my arms. Why then? Why not at some other, far more manageable, time in my life? That pivotal moment came when I received a call from someone I'd known in my old White House days.

"Hey, I heard you had a baby," she said. "That's great and all, but … uh, the executive director of my nonprofit just left. Do you still do executive search?"

A few months earlier, I'd had my moment of employment rage, leaving in a huff because the work wasn't working for me. I was disguising my unemployment as maternity leave. Sure, I knew how to do search, and I still wanted to do it. But I didn't have a vehicle through which to do it, per se.

"Well, yes," I said anyway, because all great adventures start with a bit of the unknown. And then I scrambled to put together a website, a contract, and a business suit that would fit over my postpartum derrière. I built the website myself, and I daresay it looked better than the business suit—although that was a really low bar.

Years later, when I started to guest lecture in entrepreneurship classes, I would always be asked the same question: "How long did it take you to put your business plan together?" You see, to the students looking at Present-Day Me—the highly put together, successful CEO of an executive search firm with a global portfolio (and, by then, a professional website and a suit that wasn't pushing the constraints of physics)—it appeared that my path had always been smooth sailing. That was far from the case.

My answer to this question about how long it took me to write my business plan was to ask for a piece of paper so I could write my plan right then and there. "You see, I never had a plan," I would explain. "I just had business."

I got lucky as hell with that first piece of work, but I knew that if there was to be a second or a third or a fiftieth piece of work, I'd need to hustle like mad to make it happen. I had this small alien in my arms, and he seemed to need everything from me, yet my desire to live my values through professional work hadn't changed. What had changed, however, was the importance that I placed on certain elements of my work. I had a new understanding of what would bring me consonance.

For me, flexibility suddenly became much more important than the numbers on my paycheck. The contribution that my work provided was more about how I could live my life than what I could buy in that life. Rather than a one-sided approach, seeking out clients' missions that sang to my soul, my new calling was to build a business that would do good in the world for clients who valued my work.

Control became key. Scheduling those conference calls during naptime was the dream. I was so tired all the time that I didn't have any spare energy to code-switch between my work and my personal selves. I absolutely, positively had to be in consonance. And for me to live in consonance, creating my right combination of calling, connection, contribution, and control was imperative.

Perhaps you, like me, love your work but find your workplace limiting. Perhaps the work itself is inspiring, stimulating, rewarding—but the environment in which you are working is completely the opposite.

For me, changing my workplace meant going it alone. Starting my own company began with tossing out my previous notion of what success had meant up until that point and deciding what it suddenly meant for me now. For you, it might mean going it alone—or staying where you are but with some key alterations.

It's natural to want some control over the work you do, the people with whom you do it, and the projects to which you are assigned. You want to know you have a voice in your own destiny and some agency over how you spend your time. You want to feel a direct connection between your daily tasks and the problem you are trying to solve or the bottom line you are trying to build.

With the right changes in your workplace, you could feel much more purposeful in your work. Transformation in the workplace can take several forms: from lobbying for internal modifications in your environment to going external and continuing the same type of work as a consultant or independent contractor.

Going Internal

Nicky Goren is the CEO of the Meyer Foundation, which gives to nonprofits in greater Washington, DC. The foundation was looking to shift its giving strategy to fund more diversity efforts. But Nicky knew that before the foundation could fund change externally, both she and her team had work to do internally. She tasked everyone, from the back office to the senior executives, to take part in programs that would ensure an understanding of equity and inclusion such that their work was connected to their calling, and so their work contributed to the values they wanted to live as individuals.

You, too, may find that the route to your calling is hindered by a lack of connection or contribution. You might find that you have less control over the work. Ask yourself: Are you feeling lost about how your work matters because it actually doesn't matter? Or is it because the solution you are pursuing isn't actually helping you make progress?

If your problem is the former, you probably need to bite the bullet and make that leap into an entirely new working situation, which might be an upwards and/or a lateral move into a different company or a different sector, as discussed above. On the other hand, if you simply lack the sightlines within your organization, or the agency to know or implement your usefulness, you might just need to make the ask—and take that first step toward becoming limitless.

Make the Ask

Josh Bernoff spent fifteen years at Forrester Research, doing work that he loved: researching and writing reports on the future of technology, doing expert analysis of business strategy, and then teaching others to do the same. What he loved most were the ideas and their potential. But when Forrester started going in new a direction—a direction that would have put Josh in a role that he found less interesting—he lobbied internally for the creation of a new position. The research and distillation of the Big Idea was what had always inspired Josh, so you can imagine how much he enjoyed becoming the senior vice president of idea development, and spending the next five years identifying, developing, and promoting Forrester's most powerful and influential ideas.

Many people assume that their workplace is immutable. But there is always a chance your organization will be open to making the changes you seek—if you know how to lobby correctly. Sometimes all it takes to advocate for yourself is popping up from your cubicle once in a while.

Inquire whether a supervisor has time to answer a few questions. Find a way to tag along to a meeting or two. Ask early, and ask often.

It's the only way to get what you need, especially in a workplace that feels stagnant. As an added bonus, your boss will likely see this enthusiasm as a sign of your investment in the company and your desire to step it up. He or she might loop you in more and more, which could solve the problem and help you find consonance again—without ever leaving your current seat.

You may need to be bold in making workplace demands, such as suggesting a new line of business you'd like to lead or, as Josh did, a portfolio of work you'd like to oversee. Lobbying for change can also mean using technology to bring connection, contribution, and control to your pursuit of consonance. Working from home, for example, might allow you to focus your efforts away from a limiting or uncomfortable workplace—or free you to contribute more billable hours to clients instead of spending that time in a long, unmanageable commute. Or you could ask for a budget for professional development, to control how the work contributes to your career trajectory, or for charitable matching so you can better live your values through your work.

Making the ask could change your life, so be brave! Remember, it's probably not that your employer doesn't want to offer you some new arrangement at work. More likely, he or she just didn't think of it   or didn't know that you were interested.

Take the Reins

June Smith works at a nonprofit in New York City that scouts and trains underrepresented experts to take thought leadership positions in their fields. She took the job immediately after graduating from college, feeling called to both its bold mission—to empower new voices to join the public conversation—and its leader, a dynamic female social entrepreneur.

In her first year, June worked hard to challenge herself by taking on ambitious projects and collaborating with senior leadership at the organization. She received positive informal feedback, but without a formal check-in on her performance, June was left feeling uncertain of how her work was being received and, ultimately, how it connected to her desired career trajectory.

After pushing for a review and being put off repeatedly, June made her own rubric and welcomed her team to the table in a discussion about her future at the organization. Through this enterprising and earnest process, she learned that her workplace is an environment where entrepreneurs thrive and self-advocacy is the way to win. The key to starting the conversation was to act and, in this case, evaluate her own performance and share her vision of the future.

June walked into the upcoming year knowing what she would fight for, what outcomes she wanted to see and a plan to get there, and what she deserved to earn. This shift in her perspective allowed her the space to move to an intentional mindset and positioned her as the CEO of her own portfolio.

Confronting this issue head-on can be intimidating, and especially so if you are in the early part of your career. I've known more than a few workers who left their jobs because they had no idea where they stood and couldn't get clear answers, or were afraid to ask. It's hard to plot your career course when you're out of control, when you don't have the reins.

Start by scheduling a meeting with your supervisor, and brainstorm questions to help you learn what you need to do differently to get where you want to be. Rather than leaving your workplace, become the driver in your current role. This will make it easier for your manager to let you—and even help you—grow.

Going External

Perhaps you've already tried various avenues for improving your situation at your current workplace. Perhaps work isn't working for you because you need to be working for yourself.

Leaving your workplace for external opportunities could mean forming your own company or becoming a freelancer. These options are not just for people who have had a long career. Before you think that you would be alone out there, or that you are too young, note that the pool of self-employed Americans is rising steadily, especially among the younger generations.[18]

Scott Stratten is one of them, and the only grown man I know who can pull off a man-bun. With his wife, Alison, he coauthored five best-selling books on business and entrepreneurship, and now he is a much-in-demand keynote speaker. "Entrepreneur," Scott likes to say, "is Latin for 'bad employee'." Scott simply knew, quite early in his career, that he and the nine-to-five weren't going to get along.

As a twelve-year-old, Scott happened upon a telethon on a local public television channel and was introduced to Les Brown, a legend in the motivational speaking world. Young Scott was fascinated by the idea of public speaking, and when his college education took him into human resources and training—which led him to a job with a national packaging company, traveling around North America to train its salespeople—he realized that he might be able to marry the two. (I mean, if you are getting paid to sell air, you can do pretty much anything, right?)

So Scott left that job to fulfill his calling as a keynote speaker. His first foray was a free talk at the local public library. There were seventeen people in the audience that day, nine of whom were family. The rest, he guesses, were probably just waiting for the yoga class that was to commence in the room once his talk ended.

---

18 A recent study by Deloitte found that the pool of self-employed Americans is likely to triple, reaching 42 million workers by 2020. Of those self-employed workers, 42 percent are likely to be millennials. Kelly Monahan, Jeff Schwartz, and Tiffany Schleeter, "Decoding Millennials in the Gig Economy: Six Trends to Watch in Alternative Work," *Insights* (blog), Deloitte.com, May 1, 2018, https://tinyurl.com/ycpjqnc6.

Scott started making online videos to promote his work, and when those videos went viral, he took to the road, this time speaking to larger and larger audiences. When a family medical issue forced him to stay home, he decided to make videos for others—and turned his business into one of the world's most successful viral video companies. Then the recession hit, and it went kaput.

In 2009, bankrupt except for his entrepreneurial spirit, Scott started all over again. This time he blew up on Twitter—and when he met Alison in 2010, she took his 38,000 words and turned them into the 60,000 that would become their first best-selling book. Scott is the speaker and Alison is the writer; together they are in consonance. By 2015, Scott was booking $1 million in keynote speeches.

Sure, there are sleepless nights aplenty when you start your own business. Even years on, there are always moments of uncertainty about whether the phone will ever ring again. There's the moment when your best client fires you, and the one when your worst employee just won't quit. But there is also a limitless freedom that comes with being able to decide what wars you'll wage, what battles you'll fight, and on which hills you'll be willing to die.

I found out years ago that I am a proud entrepreneur. You might be one, too.

Go It Alone

Kathy Klotz-Guest was kicking ass in Silicon Valley, with an MA and an MBA and fifteen years managing corporate marketing and communications for fast-growing high-tech companies. She was also doing comedy and improv on the side (if you count five or six nights per week as "on the side"), and pretty successfully at that. She was deeply fragmented—serious by day, funny by night. It wasn't working.

At her day job, Kathy strived to fit in, to be corporate. But it wasn't who she was. As the senior director of marketing, she was measuring her purpose by the end result, but she felt disconnected to that result both cerebrally and emotionally. Then she gave birth to her son. Her world changed.

Kathy went on maternity leave—and never went back. Her breaking point was two weeks into her maternity leave, when her boss called to ask if she could be in Japan two weeks from then. Instead of going to Japan, she resigned. Then her boss asked her to come back on a part-time basis. Rather than going back to work for him, she accepted him as the first client of her new, unplanned (and unnamed) consulting firm.

Realizing how much it mattered to be true to herself and in control of the work she did, Kathy found a way to follow her own energy. Today she makes her living as a keynote speaker; a storytelling and creativity strategist; a comedian; and an author who champions play, improv, and humor in business. No longer trying to fit into the traditional corporate environment, she is able to bring her whole self to the work she chooses. She uses her comedic chops from improv comedy and stand-up, combined with her fifteen years of corporate experience, to help people and teams be their best. She also hosts a weekly comedy show in Silicon Valley, called "Laugh Tracks," and Inc.com designated her latest book—*Stop Boring Me!*—a must-read for 2017.

As I interviewed people for this book, a recurring theme appeared time and time again: Working for yourself is one of the best ways to fulfill the elements of consonance in a combination that works for you. So think about whether it's time to call your own shots, to be your own boss. Starting a company is not for everyone, but if it makes sense for you, going out on your own could be the best choice you ever make.

Brave the Gig Economy

People shake off the bonds of the typical workplace in two distinct ways. The first is simply to leave your job and hang out a shingle, as Kathy Klotz-Guest and I both did—doing exactly what you were doing within the constraining walls of your nine-to-five, but with a better boss (mostly). The second is to leave your job but not look for the next job at all. Instead, you could look for work that is interesting, and string together enough independent projects so the combined portfolio makes for a sustainable and limitless life.

If going out on your own will enable you to find the right mix of calling, connection, contribution, and control—but you aren't ready to jump into entrepreneurship all at once—consider joining the 30 percent of the workforce already seizing their chance in the "gig economy,"[19] as described by Diane Mulcahy in her best-selling 2016 book of the same name. Being a gig economy worker isn't just moonlighting outside of your day job or doing some consulting or contractor work on the side. Truly braving the gig economy means that you depend entirely on independent gigs that, together, can financially sustain you.

Take journalism, graphic design, and athletic training as examples. In each field, full-time jobs are hard to come by simply because the cost to the employer is too high, yet there is plenty of work in the form of short-term independent gigs. As a result, these types of tasks and responsibilities are often contracted out at an hourly rate or to freelancers who work project-to-project.

Glenn Cook's career has had three chapters: He spent thirteen years writing for newspapers, almost five years in school communications, and twelve years in magazine publishing for a nonprofit. The first chapter was about learning as much as he could from a job and then moving on. The second offered insight into the complexities of an organization tasked with children's education. The third was about taking the skills he had learned in the first two chapters and applying them to a national audience.

---

19 James Manyika, Susan Lund, Jacques Bughin, Kelsey Robinson, Jan Mischke, and Deepa Mahaja, "Independent Work: Choice, Necessity, and the Gig Economy," McKinsey Institute, October 2016, https://tinyurl.com/y822uf64.

In each segment of his working life, Glenn experienced some roadblocks, from long hours to low pay to internal politics. These frustrations were counterbalanced by the fulfillment he found in being creative and in constantly learning something new—until the office environment at his last job turned toxic for his spirit. He was burned out, frustrated, drained, and disoriented about what he wanted to do and how best he should do it.

When Glenn was finally laid off in 2013, he was a forty-eight-year-old husband and father of four with limited opportunities to job hop and loads of ageism staring him in the face. Plucking the silver lining from this cloud, he cobbled together freelance work in writing and photography. Although his spouse was supportive, they were always fearful of the bottom dropping out.

Glenn stuck it out in the gig economy, and today he is engaged in more creatively fulfilling work than he could have ever imagined, using words and images to tell the stories of individuals and nonprofits. His work is broad and varied and excellent—I have a large photograph of his hanging in my office. But, above all, he only chooses projects that meet his two specific criteria: First, the project must contribute to his family by helping to pay the bills. And, second, it must contribute to his career trajectory by fulfilling his need to learn and be creative. When those criteria are met, Glenn finds connection to his clients and is able to help others and himself along the way.

For you, the consideration of whether the gig economy is the right fit for you will rest chiefly upon three things: whether your line of work caters to this type of engagement, whether you have the fortitude for the uncertainty, and whether you are able to manage without the benefits packages offered by full-time employment.

Determining Your Best Workplace Environment

So, how do you decide whether taking an internal or external path to workplace change will help you find your consonance?

We often mistake consonance for simply working within our subject matter expertise, but that is only part of the equation. Your personality and how you mesh with your colleagues, the way you go about doing your work or managing the work of others, and your general demeanor in the workplace complete the picture. Considering the right dynamic for you and how you best fit into a workplace is essential when it comes time to make a change.

Are you the type of person who operates well under pressure and in turnaround situations? Or are you better in a more stable environment where crises rarely pop up?

Are you able to get the best from working alongside legions of young, idealistic, energetic upstarts? Or are you more skilled at managing a smaller cadre of seasoned professionals?

Do you enjoy a highly charged political atmosphere at work? Or do you thrive instead in an environment where the agenda is more transparent and you're surrounded by like-minded individuals?

Discerning what type of environment brings out your best traits and allows you to flourish—and finding or creating a workplace that offers you control over that environment—will instill a stronger connection to your calling. This will enable you to work in ways that contribute to the life you want to live.

Each company, nonprofit, or entrepreneurship opportunity has its own personality and working culture. Sometimes the workplace personality reflects the organization's issue arena, its particular leadership, or the industry or sector. For example, human services nonprofits tend to be more activism-focused, with younger, idealistic staffers. Institutions of higher education tend to be more staid and steady. Start-ups are usually a buzz of 24/7 all-hands-on-deck activity. A small mom-and-pop coffee shop is a far cry from Starbucks.

Which workplace environment works best for you?

Chapter 10

Changing Yourself

If changing your career is out of the question, and changing your workplace isn't in the cards, it's time to turn the mirror back on yourself. You'll need to make some changes in terms of how you measure consonance so that you can remove the limits and become the change you need to see in your life.

Thinking back on it, you may realize you've never had consonance in your life. Or perhaps you are older now and at a different life stage, and those things that brought you consonance before are simply irrelevant now. Either way, it is up to you to determine what works for you and remove those pesky limits that have been burdening you for far too long.

There are several ways to do this. First, you have to stop trying so hard to keep up with everybody else.

Allowing Yourself to Screw the Joneses

Every fall, my social media pages are full of seemingly perfect mothers with their seemingly perfect children, all thrilled about going off to their seemingly perfect first day of school. Meanwhile, in my house, bedlam rules. It's a rare moment when my children are actually up early enough to shower (oh, puberty!) and get dressed (extra points for clean clothes!) in time to get to school—much less stand still in one place (and not roll their eyes!) long enough to bless me with that one precious, albeit cheesy, rite-of-passage photo. To wit: This year I posted a "Happy Second Day of School" photo.

It is too easy to fall into the comparison chasm, to try to keep up with the Joneses, listening to everybody's advice about what success looks like and what we must do to achieve it. And all this does is limit us. It puts everything out of whack: our understanding of the value of our calling, the connection we want to it, the contribution it gives us, and the control we need over it.

Those back-to-school photos can fill our news feeds with joy, but they—and all the other ways we fall into judging ourselves against the accomplishments of others—also fill us with pain, with endless comparisons and self-doubt. Am I doing the right thing? Did I make the right choices? What if I could have a do-over? All these prescribed definitions of success, with all of their screaming voices of perfection, contribute to the noise already in our own heads about how maybe we don't measure up, don't balance it as well, can't have it all.

It's bullshit. Every last bit of it. When we compete in the Having-It-Allympics, every last one of us loses.

Let's throw off the limiting definitions of other people's versions of success right here, right now. Politely excuse yourself from running the race someone else created for you, and start marking and running your own. Be your own dog. Make your own path. Run your own race. Judge only your own progress.

And all those voices questioning your choices and telling you what you should do and need to do? They simply don't get a vote—unless you give it to them. And that includes that voice inside your own head.

Making Hard Choices

Edison Research is the sole provider of exit polling data to the National Election Pool, the consortium of news media organizations that formed after the hanging chad debacle of the Bush–Gore 2000 election. As you might imagine, the stakes are high; the last firm with this contract went out of business immediately after that terrible call in Florida. Making mistakes is simply not an available option.

With fourteen years under his belt, Tom Webster is actually one of the shortest-tenured of the senior team at Edison. Edison is not a place of job-hoppers, because the DNA of the place allows Tom and the entire Edison team to live in complete consonance, where what they do aligns with who they are. Edison is generous with healthcare and gives to charities in the names of its employees. Edison employees have a strong moral compass ("We'd rather be last and right than first") and a strong ethical compass, and they fix errors (when they happen) quickly and with transparency. It feels good.

But it didn't always feel good for Tom. His job as senior vice president put him on the road a lot, although he didn't mind because it allowed him to deliver to clients a value set that aligned with his, which contributed to his ability to live these values in his work. On the other hand, he was noticing more and more that he did mind being home. When he was home for long stretches, he started to find all kinds of things wrong with his job, picking it apart and placing blame squarely on his work for making him unhappy.

After a while, Tom realized it wasn't his job that was broken. He was wasting time on the idea of changing jobs simply because it would be easier than changing marriages. He was trying to fix the wrong thing.

So Tom made the hard choice and figured out how to fix the right thing—his personal life—which entailed the difficult choice of divorce and the wonderful choice of remarriage. Soon he became a happier worker and a better father. His life snapped into place, where he could be in complete and total consonance.

Being Holistic

Having two sets of values—one that you are living in your work and another in your home—won't work if they are always at odds with each other. But what if each version of you supports the other, so that there is alignment between the two—or so that one enables you to do the other? Who says you have to put all your eggs in one basket?

If your primary job doesn't give you consonance, why let it fully define you? What if you flipped the script and stopped looking at your primary paid job to give you identity, purpose, and happiness—but instead looked at it as the thing that enables you to pursue that avocation you adore? Seeing your day job as the thing that contributes to how you control your connection to your calling is one of the best ways to find your consonance.

Marci Alboher, author of the highly acclaimed 2007 book *One Person/Multiple Careers*, argues that people can use a slash to incorporate their unique passions into their work. What's a slash? It's the combination of an "anchor" job—the one that pays the bills, provides the benefits, contributes to the pension, or is constrained by physical location—and an "orbit" job, or work that can be done more flexibly.

In her book, Marci describes a lawyer who works as a criminal prosecutor and is also a minister on the weekends; she also introduces a full-time high school social studies teacher who is a highly successful fashion model after three p.m., on weekends, and in the summertime. These careers seemingly have nothing in common, though mining further will probably unearth some connecting strands. A well-known example of the slash professional is Sanjay Gupta, the medical correspondent for CNN, who toggles between his on-air work and his surgery duties. This unique combination allows him to keep a hand (literally) in what's going on in clinical settings while also offering perspectives on health-related issues in the national news—with each profession informing the other.

Marci herself is a "slash," and her slashed professions evolved over time. I first got to know Marci after the publication of my previous book, *Mission Driven: Moving from Profit to Purpose*, which focuses more narrowly on the type of purpose found through cause-related nonprofit work. At the time, Marci was writing the Shifting Careers column and blog for the *New York Times*. She had spent ten years as a corporate lawyer, getting trapped by the specialization game: as a generalist, an advertising lawyer, a direct marketing lawyer, a direct mail lawyer, and finally a sweepstakes lawyer for *Reader's Digest*.

Marci was at the top of her game and was paid quite well; it helps when you are one of the top few people in the world with such a narrow specialty. But while the work was intellectually stimulating, it often felt meaningless (or even harmful), and she was hungry to shift into work that had a positive impact in the world. Because she was good at what she did and good at managing her clients, she was able to negotiate a three-day workweek—first while working in Hong Kong (so she could travel), and then with a new employer when she returned to New York (so she could take writing classes).

What Marci loved about writing was the flexibility. She could write about anything at all, but she found herself increasingly drawn to people who were pulled in several different directions at once, as she was. She traveled around the United States interviewing hundreds of slashes and eventually writing her book.

Marci's anchor job/orbit job career truly came full circle when she joined the management team at Encore.org, a nonprofit innovation hub tapping the talents of the age-fifty-plus population as a force for good. As a go-to voice on encore careers and using one's "second act" for the greater good, she has spent a lot of time delving into how people and society think about work and social purpose now that our working lives are longer than ever before. Her 2012 book *The Encore*

Career Handbook: How to Make a Living and a Difference in the Second Half of Life documents what she's learned along the way.

Marci's slash career allowed her to explore different interests, to segue into new kinds of work, and to evolve as she hit new life stages. Even though her current work is organized around one big "anchor" role at Encore, where she can marry many of her interests, she makes time for other work that orbits naturally around that focus. She's a dedicated board member at Girls Write Now, a nonprofit that mentors high school girls through writing. And she is deeply involved with other organizations doing work that matters to her—such as The OpEd Project, which amplifies and supports diverse voices in public conversation.

For Marci, it started by rejecting a singular definition of success that looks only at a workplace title. She thought about her calling, her control over how her daily work connected her to that calling, and how her "day job" contributed financially to the lifestyle she wanted and the values she held dear. By allowing herself the grace of an expanded definition—one that took into account the hours spent in her traditional job, and how those hours made space for her nontraditional jobs—Marci developed a holistic version of herself and removed the limits that were getting in her way.

As you embark on this new step of your journey, perhaps you'll find it best to keep your interests separate, like the high school teacher/model. On the other hand, you may discover a way to combine your interests, like the lawyer/minister whom Marci profiled; she later became the president of Easterseals—a nonprofit that provides support, services, and opportunities to people living with physical disabilities—while leading a community church with her husband, who is also a minister.

Could becoming a slash professional—someone who juggles some combination of an anchor job and an orbit job (or jobs)—bring you consonance?

Remixing the Balance

Jake Tedaldi's training and early employment as an in-clinic veterinarian frustrated him. He hated the constant interruptions by assistants alerting him to check on different patients. He abhorred the cold sterility of the clinical care rooms. He despised being so rushed all day long that he had to spend his evenings trying to remember which patient was which as he wrote up his charts. He had no control over the firehose of work blasting at him, disconnecting him from his calling: to provide focused care to his animal patients and their nervous caregivers.

It was only by looking at his job through the lens of fatherhood that Jake managed to perceive the way his work was limiting his ability to live in consonance. He needed to do what he loved, but he was also the father of four young sons who needed him—and the husband of a physician who worked long hours as a medical resident. So Jake came up with a plan to increase the flexibility in his working situation, which in turn afforded greater control over his daily work experience: He left the in-clinic world and started a practice as a house call vet for those pets and their nervous caregivers—me among them. Woof.

Jake found his consonance when he was able to remix his balance of the four elements. His calling and connection needed no adjustment, but he saw the need to increase his control and to recalibrate his contribution with the understanding that greater flexibility in his time made up for the dip in income. After he made the necessary change for himself—over where and how he did his work, how much or how little he worked, and how fast he grew his income and his clientele—his contribution rose to the appropriate level for him and his family.

We don't always expect or anticipate a change in what is limiting us, and often we are surprised by its effect. Typically, these changes happen as we move through certain stages, like becoming a parent or nearing retirement. But a recalibration of what consonance means to you can just as easily occur after a sudden diagnosis or a major world news story. If, at different points in your life, your needs change, so then must the values you place on calling, connection, contribution, and control.

Determining What's Right for You

Each of us will have different limits, whether external or internal, that hold us back and keep us from discovering our true path to a satisfying career and home life. You must decide what value you place on calling, connection, contribution, and control—and what personal adjustments are required so you can achieve the distinct combination that makes you limitless.

Determining what is right for you comes down to deciding one thing: What allows *what you do* to match *who you are*? Taking this introspective approach may mean asking some hard questions of yourself before you can take action and make the necessary changes.

What does success look like for you, both now and in the future?

How do you want your work to define your life or support your lifestyle?

What does your paid work allow you to do outside of working hours?

Are the values that attract you to your work the same values that you live at home?

Asking these questions will allow you to be honest with yourself about what each of the elements of calling, connection, contribution, and control mean to you.

What needs to change so you can live the life you truly want for yourself?

Conclusion

Imagine, if you will, that you have just summited Mount Everest. You trained for this feat, both mentally and physically, over many years. You spent months in crampons, climbing through snow and ice, over life-threatening crevasses, and in constant fear of avalanches, storms, and injuries. You spent countless hours preparing, organizing, fretting, dreaming. You depleted every last bit of energy through every last grueling step. And now you've reached the top. You've made it. Finally.

It's time to hang out, relax, and celebrate your success. Right?

Not exactly.

Making It Back Down Alive

In 2002, Alison Levine got an unexpected phone call. She was asked to serve as captain of the first American Women's Everest Expedition, sponsored by Ford Motor Company. Alison requested and was granted an unpaid leave of absence from Goldman Sachs, and began the training and the fundraising for this enormous endeavor. In the run-up to and throughout the adventure, Alison and her team were showcased by more than 450 media outlets, with people from across the globe eagerly awaiting news of their triumphant success.

Now, don't get it twisted. This was not some boondoggle vanity play by some corner-office Wall Street type looking for bragging rights. Alison had found herself at Goldman quite by accident. A liberal arts major from the University of Arizona and an avid outdoorswoman—she has climbed the highest peak on each of six continents, and has skied both the North Pole and the South Pole—Alison had always planned to turn her avocation into her vocation by starting an adventure travel company. She made her way to Duke University to earn an MBA and fill in the gaps on the finance and accounting side of the ledger. For a woman who took her first post-college job in pharmaceutical sales because it came with a salary of $22,000 and a company car—and she really needed that car—Goldman wasn't just a whole new world. It was a whole new universe.

But it was one that she didn't truly enjoy. Alison loved her colleagues and found the work to be challenging—so no problem there. She also appreciated the culture of reliability, accountability, and over-delivering. Yet her heart just wasn't in it. There was no connection between the work she was doing and her own calling of getting outside and exploring—and of making people's lives better by exposing them to new experiences or helping them find happiness. She felt limited.

Alison brought her massive intellect and boundless energy to work every day, but she didn't harness them to drive business results. Without connecting to her true motivations, she never reaped the kinds of rewards one might expect from a fancy Wall Street job. And she wasn't able to control her hours in a culture that demanded longer and longer working days—inside at a desk rather than in the Great Outdoors.

So when that phone call came in 2002 inviting Alison to captain the all-women expedition up Mount Everest, she jumped at the chance. She was heading for the top of the world.

And she almost made it, too.

Alison's team was 275 feet from the top of a 29,029-foot mountain when the weather changed. Success was within their grasp, but quickly slipping through their fingers. Alison knew that continuing to the summit would come with the fatally high likelihood of never getting back down again. As the captain, she was faced with making the call, and she knew the team had to turn around. They had everything it took, but Mother Nature took everything they had.

Improbably, in 2010, Alison found herself back on Everest, a place she never thought she'd revisit. This time she was at the summit, holding an ice ax engraved with the name *Meg*, honoring a friend who had died too young from complications of the flu just five months earlier, after beating lymphoma twice. Alison stood on the summit just long enough to pull out a T-shirt emblazoned with the words "Team Meg" and smile broadly for a photo to commemorate the moment. Then she high-fived the rest of her team, turned around, and headed back down the Great White Monster.

Wait, what?

She didn't stay up there for hours and celebrate finally succeeding?

No, because staying on the summit for much longer than that brief moment would only further deplete her oxygen and endanger her climb down. But, more importantly, Alison didn't linger at the top because she'd already succeeded the first time.

It turns out that success isn't what we think it is—in reality, the traditional definitions don't cut it. Success in your career isn't filling up a bucket of gold stars or landing a perfect-on-paper job or marking all the checkboxes set out by others. Success isn't getting to the top of Mount Everest. It's getting back down to the bottom, alive.

Alison did that—twice. And even though she still doesn't run that outdoor exploration company (yet!), her work traveling around the world, imparting lessons about management and leadership learned throughout her own adventures, now brings her consonance. She is able to fulfill her calling by helping people become better versions of themselves. She understands how each talk to each audience connects to that calling. And she is one of the most highly paid women on the speaking circuit, allowing her some control over her working schedule. Meanwhile, she lives her values and enjoys a better level of financial contribution than she could through the pharmaceutical company car or her mediocre Goldman performance.

As Alison describes in her best-selling 2014 book, *On the Edge: Leadership Lessons from Mount Everest and Other Extreme Environments*, sometimes it takes turning around to go forward.

Stepping Off the Beaten Path

Likewise, sometimes moving forward takes stepping off the path altogether. Jack Lew did just that.

Like many young idealists, Jack started off as an intern on Capitol Hill. He was a child of the 1960s who spent his time in high school petitioning his principal to stop the war in Vietnam, volunteering on many election campaigns, organizing participation in the first Earth Day, and coordinating the New York March on Hunger. All of these actions reflected his lifelong, unwavering belief that each and every one of us can and should do something to make this world a better place.

Jack's early jobs were as an aide in various congressional offices and in Boston city government. Since then, he has spent his career moving back and forth between private- and public-sector work. He served as executive director of the House Democratic Steering and Policy Committee for Speaker Thomas P. O'Neill, Jr., working there from 1979 until the speaker retired in 1987. That's when Jack left the Hill to practice energy law.

I met Jack in 1993, when he came back into government to help write the legislation that would become AmeriCorps. People asked why he was interested; he'd already had a Big Job on the Hill, after all. Why would he want to go work for a small office in the White House that was going to start a nice little program (if it could make its way through Congress) that would not come close to the large-scale policy issues he was accustomed to working on?

Jack was guided then by the same principle that guides his career to this day: Do interesting work with good people. While everyone defines the terms *interesting work* and *good people* differently, for Jack it was about creating a structure in which each of us, through service, could improve our communities and our country. Plus, he just plain liked Eli Segal, the director of our office, from the moment they met. Jack knew the program mattered, and he trusted that Eli would look out for his best interests. He figured the worst thing that could happen would be spending eight or nine months doing something that was important to him, even if it had little to do with the rest of his career. Then he would get back onto a more familiar path.

If you recognize the name Jack Lew, it's because his signature is probably on some of the bills in your wallet right now. Listening to his self-determined definition of success, Jack embarked on what would become a storied career path in the White House—as director of the Office of Management and Budget under President Bill Clinton and then President Barack Obama, as deputy secretary for Hillary Clinton when she ran the US State Department, as chief of staff for President Obama—and eventually as the 76th Secretary of the United States Treasury.

Jack didn't know the Clintons or the Obamas before he started working for Eli. He didn't seek that nice little job for that nice little program in order to position himself for future gain. He just knew that by listening to his own guiding principle—*Do interesting work for good people*—his world of experience and opportunity would expand and, along with it, the likelihood that future opportunities that fit his guiding principle would arise. Jack didn't have a specific plan about what his career would be when he embarked on day one of his first job, or on any of his subsequent positions, for that matter. And he certainly did not foresee his next step after coming to work on Ameri-Corps, which became a signature program of the Clinton administration, and which has won bipartisan support while giving more than one million people the opportunity to serve their community and their country.

The idea of national and community service called to Jack, and he loved the idea of a program that could give structure to the movement. He was inspired by the leadership with which he'd be working every day and the president under whom he would serve.

He had connection. As the chief author of the legislation, Jack had a direct line of sight into how each decision he made would affect the bill's eventual chances of passage and enshrinement into law. And as one of the chief advocates, traveling around the country to get national and statewide elected officials on board, his ability to communicate his choices was crucial.

He had contribution. This work allowed the values of service in Jack's life to define his work. He put himself in a smaller office but in a bigger operation, which increased his optionality for future opportunities. The world of people who recognized his contributions grew to include the president and senior leadership in the White House.

He had control. Even though the fulfillment of this campaign promise was one of the first out of the gate of President Clinton's first administration, and even though the work was fast and furious, Jack was working with people who respected that he had a young family and had important commitments to them as well. I recall a time when Jack and Eli were traveling state to state, selling the program to governors, but Eli still made sure to get Jack home in time to celebrate Shabbat with his family.

That combination of calling, connection, contribution, and control in his role had a lasting impact on Jack. He later founded and chaired the board of City Year New York and served on the board of the Corporation for National and Community Service. Today, he serves on the advisory board of Service Year and is a frequent advocate for AmeriCorps funding. And despite subsequently serving in much Bigger Jobs, Jack says AmeriCorps still holds an important place in his heart.

*　*　*　*　*

Alison turned around. Jack stepped away. Both of them offer inspiring success stories, although neither followed the expected path. They *achieved* success because of how they *defined* success. They determined and pursued their own levels of calling, connection, contribution, and control that would lead to their personal consonance. And in doing so, they became limitless.

Now, it's your turn.

Acknowledgments

Arthur Ashe once said, "Start where you are, use what you have, do what you can."

I have done what I can because I had all of you, and you accepted me for where I was and made me a better version of myself.

Tamsen Webster, you recognized that I had a Big Idea and asked me to consider doing a TEDx talk, which led to an unplanned speaking career, an invitation into a community of world-class humans, and introductions to a number of people who would be instrumental in the creation of this book. Scott Stratten, you are a man-bunned prince among men; you did good, and you married way the hell up, too. Rohit Bhargava, you took a chance on my idea and recognized that it could be bigger. Daniel Lemin, your early read set the ship in the right direction. Carey Lohrenz, you handed me my ass in the kindest possible way, and didn't let me get away with mediocrity; you and Alison Levine are the best wolf pack any woman could have. Clay Hebert, the brilliance you laid out in forty-five minutes was the biggest turning point of the book, its trajectory, its energy, and its vibe. And most of all, Mitch Joel, you are truly the godfather of this book; your advice, pep talks, and well-couched criticism made me dig deep to get it right. (This book is truly a Speak & Spill Production.)

To my family sister Caren Krumerman and my framily sister Ilona Goldfarb, to Beneva Nyandebo, Richard Tagle, Rayanne Thorn, Michelle Hynes, Karen Wright, Ted "C." Hammerman, Daniel McConvey, Gretchen Gardner, and Amy Dorta McIlwaine—your repeated reading, commenting, and editing made my ideas live up to their potential.

To my friends who listened to me (endlessly) as I worked out my ideas on runs, on ERGs, at stadiums—you may now return to your noise-canceling earphones. To my friends who got the same treatment over dinners and drinks—the next round is on me.

To my parents, who recognized my crisis of consonance all those years ago—I'll never understand how you found the flexibility to let me take such a flyer, drop out of law school, and join a presidential campaign for an unknown guy from Arkansas, but I'm sure glad you did. And, to my inlaws, the best a girl could want, thank you for modeling for me a life of purpose.

To my children, Benjamin and Tobias, who influence me more than they will ever know, and who inspire me more than I ever thought possible—I am so lucky to be your mom.

To my husband, Jonathan, whose brilliance is surpassed only by his undying patience—you are my home. Thanks for keeping the dog alive while I wrote.

To those who lent me their stories, who themselves bravely made the changes they needed to make to live their own lives of consequence, I salute you.

And to you, the reader, who put your trust in me—I believe in you, and I can't wait to see what you do next.